With best wishes -
Eddie Merrins

Playing
a Round
with
the Little Pro

Playing a Round with the Little Pro

A Life in the Game

Eddie Merrins
with Mike Purkey

With a Foreword by Byron Nelson

ATRIA BOOKS

NEW YORK LONDON TORONTO SYDNEY

ATRIA BOOKS

1230 Avenue of the Americas
New York, NY 10020

Library of Congress Cataloging-in-Publication Data

Merrins, Eddie.
Playing a round with the Little Pro :
a life in the game / Eddie Merrins ; with Mike Purkey.
p.   cm.
1. Merrins, Eddie.   2. Golfers—United States—Biography.
3. Golf.   I. Purkey, Mike.   II. Title.
GV964.M47A3   2006
796.352092—dc22
[B]   2005057193

ISBN-13: 978-0-7432-7425-8
ISBN-10: 0-7432-7425-3

First Atria Books hardcover edition April 2006

10   9   8   7   6   5   4   3   2   1

ATRIA BOOKS is a trademark of Simon & Schuster, Inc.

Manufactured in the United States of America

For information about special discounts for bulk purchases,
please contact Simon & Schuster Special Sales at
1-800-456-6798 or business@simonandschuster.com.

Here's to all of you, with love

Foreword

EDDIE MERRINS IS AS ACCOMPLISHED A PGA GOLF PROFESSIONAL as I have known. His path from junior golf to his present status as golf professional emeritus at Bel-Air has been truly noteworthy.

We first had the opportunity to meet at the Jaycee International Junior Championship in 1949 at the Houston Country Club, where I gave a golf clinic. He was sixteen. Eddie won that championship the next year, defeating Gay Brewer in the finals.

The following year, he and I played in a golf exhibition foursome match in Brookhaven, Mississippi. His 68 was the low score.

College at LSU saw Eddie compete against the North Texas State team that I helped with Coach Fred Cobb in the early '50s. He individually won the Southern Intercollegiate in 1953 and the Southeast Conference Championship in 1953–54, and was second to Jim Vickers in the 1952 NCAA Championship.

As an amateur golfer, Merrins three times won the Mississippi Amateur and was second in the Southern Amateur, the Southwest Amateur, and the All American Championship at Tam O'Shanter in Chicago. He won the prestigious Western

Amateur in 1955, defeating Hillman Robbins Jr. in the finals. As an amateur of twenty-one, he won the Gulf Coast Open in Gulfport, Mississippi, and played in four USGA Amateur Championships before turning pro.

Turning pro at age twenty-four in 1957, Eddie served his PGA apprenticeship at some of this country's great clubs: Merion, Thunderbird, Westchester, and Rockaway Hunt. His forty-plus years at Bel-Air have been a great romance, which saw him receive practically every award possible as a PGA professional.

His career had him compete in two hundred tour events plus six club pro championships, eight U.S. Opens, and six PGA championships. I encountered him at a number of these events when I worked with Chris Schenkel on ABC television golf coverage.

We also worked together in various charity events like Cy Laughter's Bogey Busters in Dayton (where I met my wife, Peggy) and Friends of Golf (FOG) in Los Angeles at Bel-Air in an event founded by Eddie. Both of these events of over twenty years' duration served to raise a lot of money for worthy causes. He has always had an affinity for amateur golf, which groomed his beginning. An ardent supporter of the USGA, Merrins also participated in the goodwill program People to People and made guest instructional appearances worldwide. He helped to establish the World Club Championships (WCC), featuring selected clubs from *Golf Magazine*'s listing of the World's Top 100.

Coaching the UCLA Golf Team for fourteen years (1975–89) offered Eddie Merrins the opportunity to utilize his talents as player, teacher, fund-raiser, and professional. This program was recently cited by *Golf Digest* as the number one college golf program in America. Eddie and his friends had a lot to do with this. Several of his players are excelling on the tour today. Three of college golf's most prestigious awards are due largely to the efforts of Eddie Merrins: the Ben Hogan Trophy, the Byron Nelson Award, and the Dinah Shore Trophy.

The Little Pro, as he is affectionately known, has contributed mightily to golf instruction with his books, videos, articles, and appearances. At this stage of his life he is devoting his efforts toward helping others improve their lot in golf. Whatever ranking he derives as a teacher is well earned.

Having known Lisa Merrins on the golf course as well as off, I know where Eddie gets his drive. She's a pistol! Their two boys, Michael and Mason, represent them well. His religious devotion is obvious in his relationships, family and otherwise.

I am glad to share with you my insights into a unique individual. Eddie's contributions to the game have come from in-depth experiences in every area of involvement. His willingness to share this reservoir is a typical example of his lifetime of giving as well as living. Enjoy what you are about to receive!

Byron Nelson
Roanoke, Texas

A Dawning

ONE GLORIOUS AUGUST MORNING IN 1976, THE SUN WAS RISING over an awakening Los Angeles with its beautiful rays sparkling off the dew on our first holes at Bel-Air. The fairways were roped and defined, the rough was tidy, the bunkers and greens were inviting. Our course was ready to host the seventy-sixth U.S. Amateur Championship in the bicentennial-year celebration of our country. As I soaked in the realization of this moment in my early morning solitude, a few tears of joy and appreciation appeared with the realization that I was part of this scene. Let me share my story.

I think I'm the luckiest man on the face of the earth. My life in golf has been nothing short of magical. I have turned a boyhood passion into a lifelong dream come true. I have played golf with Ben Hogan, Sam Snead, Gene Sarazen, and Byron Nelson. I played alongside Arnold Palmer and Jack Nicklaus. I arranged for Nicklaus and fifteen-year-old Tiger Woods to meet for the first time. I count them, as well as many others, among my friends.

I came to Bel-Air Country Club in 1962 as the head golf professional and I have kept regular hours there ever since. In almost fifty years of teaching, since 1957, I've given more than forty thousand golf lessons, from celebrities to PGA Tour players to rank beginners and everything in between.

And I've done most of it at one of the best clubs in the world. The head golf professional's job at Bel-Air is one of the most prestigious there is in our profession. Of course, any job is what you make it, but the people of Bel-Air have treated my family and me like, well . . . family. The thing I respect most about the membership here is that I have been allowed to grow with my family with dignity. We have enjoyed the privileges of this club, and our guests can come here and be treated royally. The members here consider me more than just an employee—not many people in my profession can say that.

When I quit playing the PGA Tour full-time in 1962, my life changed. It became a life of service. For the past couple of years, I have come out of the golf shop and am now the pro emeritus at Bel-Air. You can either be put out to pasture in such a position or you can take the opportunity to do things that might be more important than anything you've done before.

Giving back to the game is what I enjoy doing. If I don't play another round of golf, I will have played enough golf. I'd be satisfied about that. But I'd like to teach until I drop because I feel as though I'm helping someone to help himself. It's not like you're coming up with a cure for cancer, but you are helping your fellow man. Millions of people play this game, and they want to play better. I can help them do that.

We live in a world that's full of stress and turmoil, but if there's something I can do to help people temporarily forget about those troubles and enjoy themselves, then I've done something worthwhile.

The key, of course, is giving unconditionally. I've always been taught that if you give something away, it comes back tenfold. It's amazing how that is the case as long as you give with no strings attached. It comes back in ways you never expect.

During my time at Bel-Air, I have taught celebrities, famous coaches, and athletes what I know about the golf swing. Along the way, I have reached millions of other golfers through magazine articles, my book *Swing the Handle,* and my video series of the same name.

In this book, you will learn about my teaching philosophy and my life experiences that helped shape me as a player, a teacher, and a person, and you will meet some of the people I've known who have made my life all the richer. No one is more fortunate—or more grateful—than I am.

Bing and the Snake

I DON'T KNOW OF MANY PEOPLE WHO LOVED THE GAME OF GOLF and everything that went with it more than Bing Crosby did. What's more, he gave back to the game ten times—maybe more—what he received from it. His legacy lives on at the AT&T Pebble Beach National Pro-Am, one of the best-known tournaments in the world and one that carried his name from the beginning.

Bing played most of his golf at Lakeside, Cypress Point, Burlingame, and Bel-Air. You could tell Bing was coming by the trail of pipe smoke that preceded him. He was quite an accomplished player, having once played in the British Amateur.

When he played at Bel-Air, he had a regular caddie—a man named Arnold who was called "Snake." Snake was a self-promoter, always looking for a deal from one of the members or the other caddies that would directly benefit him. He had a standing arrangement with Crosby whereby if Bing scored under par, he would buy Snake a new suit.

One summer day, Bing—with quite an assist from Snake—shot a 1-under-par 69. Leaving the eighteenth green and walking through the tunnel to the elevator beneath the Bel-Air clubhouse, Snake proposed a deal, probably because he had all the suits he needed and was looking for something this day that spent a little easier.

"Bing, if it's just the same to you," Snake said, "I'll take cash today because my tailor is on vacation."

When Crosby died in 1977 near Madrid, he, who was the master at stage presence, could not have orchestrated his final act better. He had just finished his round of golf at a local course, and he and the club professional eked out a 1-up victory over two others. They were en route from the eighteenth green to celebrate in the clubhouse when Bing collapsed and died.

Along the way, during the last round of his life, Bing sang his last song, when he encountered a group of Spanish golf course workers in midround. They were having their lunch in the shade of the twelfth hole. He joined them for a chorus of "Spanish Eyes." We should all take our final bow that way.

Tiger Woods

WE HAD LITTLE IDEA IN APRIL 1991 THAT A MEETING BETWEEN A high schooler and the greatest player who ever lived would serve as a symbolic passing of the baton from one golf generation to the next. Tiger Woods met Jack Nicklaus for the first time at our Friends of Golf outing at Bel-Air, but it wasn't until sometime later that those in attendance realized what a historic occasion they had witnessed.

Nicklaus had agreed to be the Friends of Golf honoree that year, and Byron Nelson was on hand to lend further greatness to the occasion. Dinah Shore, our "First Lady of FOG," was also in attendance.

On the Sunday before the Monday event, Nicklaus flew by helicopter from his office in Columbus, Ohio, to Dayton to the site of one of his new courses. On the return flight, they encountered fog and had to set down in a farmer's field. The friendly farmer came to the aid of his newfound guests and was excited to learn that Jack Nicklaus had come to visit. After all, how often does the world's greatest golfer come to call?

The farmer took his guests to the house and proudly introduced them to his less-than-impressed wife. "I thought you had brought someone famous," she deadpanned. "Like [Indy car driver] Bobby Rahal." With ego intact, Nicklaus made his way back to Columbus and successfully arrived at Bel-Air the following morning.

We had invited a young man named Phil Mickelson to

represent college and amateur golf. At the time, he was the NCAA champion and the U.S. Amateur champion. Bel-Air member Terry Jastrow, who was the ABC director responsible for U.S. Open golf coverage for twenty years, brought a film crew. He saw an opportunity to record the changing of the guard with Nicklaus and Mickelson in attendance at the same prestigious event.

At the last minute, however, Mickelson was forced to cancel his appearance, which left a high school student from nearby Cypress named Eldrick "Tiger" Woods to find himself front and center with the great Nicklaus. Young Tiger, accompanied by his father, Earl, had been invited to represent high school and junior golf. He was fifteen at the time and his junior golf career was just beginning to blossom. Little did we know at the time that this was the "Bear Apparent."

During the golf clinic that preceded the afternoon of golf, Tiger was the first onstage as Jastrow's crew was busy recording the moment for posterity on videotape. I asked him to hit some 3-iron shots and explain to the gathering the cause and effect of the beautiful shots they were seeing. I realize that asking a youngster to hit 3-irons in front of a crowd that included Jack Nicklaus and Byron Nelson was a bit daunting, but Tiger handled the request with a manner beyond his years. Not to mention that he hit every 3-iron shot right in the center of the clubface.

Steve Pate and Duffy Waldorf, two of my former UCLA players, did a fade-and-draw midair crisscross before they turned the stage over to Nicklaus. It takes a lot to impress Jack, so this next comment was well measured. "Tiger," he said, "you might win as many Masters as Arnold [Palmer] and I combined." And this was after seeing Tiger for the first time.

Nicklaus played nine holes that afternoon, and except for one pushed tee shot out of bounds on the ninth hole when Jastrow tempted him to try to drive the par-4 green, he was still hitting every shot perfectly like the Nicklaus of old, even at age fifty-one.

Tiger was paired that day with Dinah Shore, along with Bel-Air members John Marin and Jim Middleton with Arco President Lod Cook. At the par-5 fourteenth hole, playing 565 yards from the regular tee, the fifteen-year-old Woods hit the green with his 3-iron second shot. I guess that 3-iron warm-up at the clinic paid off.

This day belonged to us all because the two players who might be recorded as the greatest of all time had the opportunity to get to know one another for the first time. Each was duly impressed.

At the conclusion of the evening's FOG festivities, young Tiger sought out my wife and me and politely thanked us for having invited him to the occasion. Lisa smiled and said, "Now, Tiger, did your mom and dad have you say that?"

"Yes, Mrs. Merrins," he admitted with a grin.

Quizzed by the Bear

ON THE EVE OF THE 1978 BRITISH OPEN, I WAS standing on the practice tee at St. Andrews, working and chatting with Tom Kite. At that moment, over sidled the great Jack Nicklaus. And he looked straight at me.

"You believe in swinging the handle, don't you?" he asked.

"Well, yes I do," I replied, wondering what he had in mind.

"Explain that to me," Nicklaus said.

One of golf's four major championships is about to commence in less than twenty-four hours and the greatest player ever to have played the game is asking me to explain my teaching philosophy. What was I going to say?

Out of the blue, I remembered that Nicklaus liked to play tennis. "Swing the handle is simply a two-armed tennis stroke," I told him. "That's the best analogy I know. Both forearms combine to swing the handle of the racket from one side of your body to the other. You do the same thing when you make a good golf swing."

Nicklaus thought about it for a minute, then went back to his spot on the practice tee and continued to hit his pile of balls. Now, I don't know what he might have thought about what I said, for he has not asked me about it since. But I do know that he won that British Open. I have no idea if anything I said made a sliver of difference, but I liked the fact that the holder of eighteen major championships was still curious as to whether there is a better, simpler, easier way to swing a golf club.

I happen to think the entire philosophy of the golf swing is embodied in "Swing the Handle." When I was an assistant at Merion in the 1950s, I really didn't care about how to swing the club. I didn't have any formal golf training as a youngster; I learned to play by feel and instinct. I didn't want to work on my swing. I just wanted to play.

By playing regularly at Merion, one of the architecturally finest courses in the world, I learned the fine art of shot making. I knew how to hit fades and draws, high shots and low ones, grass shots and bunker shots, run-up shots and wind shots, you name it. I knew what to do, I just didn't know how to do it. And I certainly didn't know how to tell anyone else how to do it.

But I was being asked to teach lessons and I thought I had better learn how to do that well. I knew about grip and setup, but I really didn't know about swinging the club. I wanted to be able to convey that information in the simplest way possible.

In the late '50s, all teaching was about the hands and clubhead. All of a sudden, it occurred to me that you don't actually swing that end of the club. I came to see that you swing the handle end of the club. I never called it the "butt" of the club; that didn't appeal to me. I prefer the "handle" or, more precisely, the "hub" of the club.

The swing is created at the hub of the club. There are two

arcs in the swing: the outer arc and the inner arc. I thought that the inner arc—that created by the handle—is the one that truly matters and the one over which we have the most control. If you are in control of the inner arc, you are in control of the outer arc. But it doesn't work the other way around.

I began to see that this could really be the secret to the golf swing because everything you see happening with the swing begins and ends at the handle. The swing starts at the handle, it continues there, it accelerates there, and it stops there. You determine the length of the swing with the handle, you determine the tempo, the timing, and the rhythm. You do it all with the handle.

It's the principle of the wheel. When any kind of wheeled vehicle moves, it doesn't go anywhere unless the hub of the wheel moves. The rest of the wheel is attached to the hub. The spokes, the rim, the tire, the vehicle all move accordingly, and the faster the hub moves, the faster the vehicle moves. When you want it to stop, the brake mechanism slows the hub down and the vehicle comes to a stop.

That's exactly what happens in a golf swing. If you want to apply speed to the clubface, you do so at the handle. When you slow it down, you do so at the hub. When the hub comes to rest, the club should be full rested. Because there had been no teaching referring to the handle end of the club, as far as I was concerned I had made a discovery that others didn't know about. In my own mind, I had found the secret to the golf swing.

So I became my own guinea pig. I played using my theory and I played well enough to compete with the best players in the world. In my own mind, I felt that I truly knew some things the rest of the players didn't know. In that sense, I had more confidence than even I realized. I felt that I really knew what I was doing. To me, that's a big advantage. And I began to translate my newfound discoveries to the Merion members.

Fred Austin was the head professional at Merion at the time. Remarkably, he had never played a round of golf. But he was a devotee of Ernest Jones, one of golf's all-time great teachers. Jones advocated swinging the clubhead, and his favorite drill was to attach a penknife to the end of a handkerchief and have the student hold one end of the cloth while swinging that knife back and forth. When the hands and knife were swinging together, Jones believed, you had the right prescription for the golf swing.

To Austin's credit, he never insisted that I teach that way, even though he was thoroughly convinced that Jones was right. That's why I have never forced any assistant who worked for me to employ my theory in his or her teaching. I'll be glad to answer any question they have, but I don't insist they do it my way. Let them do it their way.

Like Fred Austin, I am equally convinced that my way is the right way. It's been very, very rare when I've left a lesson with the feeling that I didn't help the person I was instructing. After nearly every lesson I've ever given, I've felt that I've offered the student more than what he bargained for. He got what he wanted and then some.

Growing Up

MERIDIAN, MISSISSIPPI, WAS A WONDERFUL PLACE FOR A BOY TO grow up in the 1930s and '40s. It was a farming community that lay on a little crossroads, midway between Jackson and Birmingham, right on the Alabama line. Its remote, country location made life simple.

I was born and raised there and lived there for my first twenty-four years. Like most red-blooded American boys, I was exposed to all the usual sports, especially football and baseball. I was captain of my junior high baseball team. I played those sports when I entered high school, but by that time I had been smitten with a new love—golf.

During the summer that I turned eleven years old, I was exposed to golf by some young friends who had access to the one club in Meridian, a place called Northwood Country Club. I was so taken with the game that my parents, in self-defense, had to figure out a way to join the club in order to support my new habit. Every day after school, I headed directly to the golf course. I gave up the other sports because golf occupied every minute of spare daylight.

By the time I was thirteen, I was scoring in the 70s. At fourteen, I qualified for the Mississippi State Amateur. One of the reasons I bloomed so far so fast is that the men of the club took me into their fold. They invited me to play in their games, where we'd have games of chance that involved quarters and half-dollars, big money in those days, especially for a fourteen-year-old.

Their friendship and guidance were invaluable. These men of Northwood took me to play in tournaments, invitational-type events within a two-hundred-mile radius of Meridian, and I was fortunate enough to compete against players much better and much older than I was. I learned about playing and competing in such a short period of time and at such a young age that I grew up (in golf years) much faster than some of my contemporaries might have.

I'll never forget my compadres who helped start me in the game—Neal Watts, Dick Lyle, Mac McAllister, and Bubsie Patty. In the beginning, we were constant companions. My first junior championship at the club, I lost in the final to Bubsie. He was older, but the defeat still hurt. We used to play little competitive games, like one that we called Short Man Chase.

We didn't have a driving range at Northwood in those days, but we had a practice tee near the ninth green where you hit your shag balls down the fairway and then went to pick them up. There sometimes were ten of us on the tee and we all hit shots and the player who hit the ball the shortest distance had to go and pick up all the balls and bring them back. Then we had putting games and we tried to encourage one another to practice as much as possible. To tell the truth, I didn't practice as much as some of my friends as a young-ster because I preferred playing golf, believing it to be more beneficial than just hitting hundreds of balls on the driving range. I thought my development as a player would be better served by trying to shoot as low a score as I could and trying to avoid losing in a match-play situation.

When I was seventeen and a senior in high school, I won the state junior championship, the state high school championship, and, that summer, the Mississippi State Amateur. That same year, I went to the quarterfinals of the Southern Amateur in New Orleans and won the Jaycee National Junior Championship in Ames, Iowa, beating Gay Brewer in the finals. Brewer at the time was the defending USGA Junior champion. He and I had quite a match over thirty-six holes, which I won 1-up.

But none of that held quite the thrill of an event later that summer, when I was privileged to play an exhibition with the great Byron Nelson in Brookhaven, Mississippi, about fifty miles from Jackson. I shot 68 to Nelson's 71 and was the low score in the foursome. I was ecstatic. The feat garnered some local publicity at the time, and it was a great accomplishment for one so young. However, in no way did I get the impression that I was as good as Byron Nelson. It was gratifying to have performed so well under those conditions. But as good as Nelson? Even at seventeen, I knew better than that.

Lord Byron

BYRON NELSON IS AS MUCH A GENTLEMAN GOLFER AS ANY FAMOUS player who has ever graced our game. I have a lifetime of admiration for Byron, going back to the time I took up the game at age eleven. In that magic year of 1945, he was in the midst of his great streak of eleven straight PGA Tour victories and a total of eighteen wins, a feat that will never be equaled.

Not only was he a World Golf Hall of Fame player, he was just as much a friend to those close to him. He was a mentor to Ken Venturi and Tom Watson, both of whom he helped immeasurably. They both credit much of their success to Nelson and hold him in nothing short of reverence.

I hold him in equally high esteem and always have. We have been together on numerous occasions over the years, most particularly the Masters, the U.S. Open, and the PGA Championship. We were on the *Golf Digest* Teaching Panel together, and he has graced our presence at the Friends of Golf day we hold at Bel-Air each year.

In 1987, the FOG honored Arnold Palmer's achievements in the game, and Nelson was on hand for the festivities. But it was under some tragic circumstances that Nelson joined us that year. Shortly before he came to Los Angeles, his beloved wife, Louise, had died. He was as sad and downhearted as I've ever seen anyone.

Fortunately, when one door closes, another opens, and a year later, Nelson met a wonderful woman named Peggy at the Bogey Busters in Dayton. They married, and he wore a perpetual smile at the 1988 FOG when we honored Greg Norman. They are very much in love, even to this day, and are a model couple. I couldn't be happier for them both.

A favorite memory is that of a warm, sunny Los Angeles day at the 1992 FOG at Bel-Air when he patiently signed three hundred copies of his book *How I Played the Game*, which Peggy worked so diligently with him to produce.

Another memory is of Byron sitting behind the eighteenth green at Los Colinas during the Byron Nelson Classic and greeting every player on the completion of his round. Each competitor is made to feel important. It is no wonder that this event has proved to be the biggest charity fund-raiser in all of sport. A bronze likeness of Nelson, Texas-style, towers over the clubhouse area at Los Colinas. It is fitting indeed for a man whose contributions are so bountiful.

In 1996 at Los Colinas, during play of the Eleven in a Row, a pro-member event dedicated to the memory of Byron's streak of 1945, a tender moment ensued. My wife, Lisa, and I were paired with Peggy and Byron. During the course of this delightful round, Byron had a 40-foot birdie putt on the fifth hole and left the approach putt some 12 feet short of the cup.

Lisa, no shy wallflower, stated, "Byron, that was a half nelson!"

The last word is not something that Byron relished but at times called for, as was the case in 1995 at the PGA Merchandise Show in Orlando. Nelson was being feted by the Cleveland Golf Company, which he represented, on the fiftieth anniversary of his magnificent year.

Sam Snead was invited to be a spokesman for the occasion. In his inimitable fashion, Snead recounted tales of their years of competition on the tour. In summary, he announced to Byron in front of the audience that surely the '45 record was great, but he, Snead, had a lot more fun through the years.

Given his opportunity to speak, Byron complimented

Snead on his fabulous play, then seized the moment. "Sam, if you don't think winning eighteen tournaments was fun, what do you think it was?"

One thing that most people don't know about Byron is that in the late '40s and early '50s, golf coach Fred Cobb of North Texas State wisely enlisted the services of Byron to help train his young players. NTS won the NCAA Championship four years in a row, from 1949 to 1952. Included among those players were 1951 U.S. Amateur Champion Billy Maxwell, 1953 British Amateur winner Joe Conrad, and 1967 PGA Champion Don January. Obviously Byron was a factor in producing these victories.

Sitting next to Don Spencer of the USGA at Byron's eightieth birthday celebration in Dallas, I learned a story the likes of which I had never heard. In 1956, during dinner at Pebble Beach, Eddie Lowery, who caddied for Francis Ouimet when Ouimet beat Harry Vardon and Ted Ray in the 1913 U.S. Open, boasted to good friend George Coleman of Oklahoma and Seminole that his two amateur employees Ken Venturi and Harvie Ward could beat any two other golfers in a better-ball match.

Coleman took the bait and suggested to Lowery that for a sizable sum of money he would have two players show up at Cypress Point the following week to take on Venturi, who had recently led the Masters until a last-round 80 caused him to finish second to Jackie Burke by 1 shot, and Ward, who was the current U.S. Amateur champion. Surely they were the two best young amateurs in the world.

Eager to know who the opposition was to be, Lowery

gulped when Coleman stated that his two players would be Nelson and Ben Hogan.

I had the opportunity to quiz these participants, and the facts were verified by all four. What took place was better than anything Hollywood could have staged. On one of the world's greatest courses, this stellar foursome was a combined 27 under par. The match was all even through the fifteenth hole, then Nelson birdied the great par 3 sixteenth for his team to go 1-up. Both teams birdied seventeen, and Venturi rolled in a 15-foot putt for birdie at eighteen that might have tied the match.

Hogan, left with a curling 6-footer, conferred with Byron, and a decision was made not to lose to these young amateurs. Ben holed this putt for the win.

During a rain delay in the 2003 Colonial at Fort Worth, I had the opportunity to go with my friend Dr. Bill Barnes to visit with Byron at his ranch in Roanoke, which he bought in 1945 with his money winnings of that year. He told people that his motivation that season was to accumulate enough money to buy that ranch.

It might be the most well-earned piece of property in golf.

David Feherty

GOLF NEEDS MORE OF WHAT DAVID FEHERTY has to offer. He is a learned player, having had a successful European Tour career, and he is a student of the game. But he is also one of the funniest people in golf and introduces humor to a game that some say can be pretty bland.

David was the master of ceremonies for my *Swing the Handle* video series and also appears in Volume IV, "Playing the Game," where he serves as the student.

It is fitting that Feherty appeared in "Playing the Game" because he did it so well. As a European Tour member and a Ryder Cup team member, he learned how to play different shots at different times. He wasn't a one-dimensional player. And that's what playing the game well is all about.

Most instruction leaves you on the practice tee with a pile of balls in front of you, some ideas about the swing and technique, and perhaps some information about hitting certain shots. But it doesn't take you beyond the practice tee.

In the making of the video, David and I explored the difference between goals and rewards. There are four goals: the shot at hand, the hole you are playing, the eighteen-hole round, and the entire tournament. The score you shoot is not a goal; it is a reward for how you played each shot that adds up to a score on a hole and each hole that adds up to a score for a round. Winning is not a goal; it is a reward for how you played each shot, each hole, and each round of the tournament.

When you tee off, you don't have any idea what your score is going to be, so it's a mistake to be thinking score when you play. If you relate well to each goal, you will play well and be rewarded. Had Greg Norman figured that out, he never would have lost a 6-stroke lead at the Masters in 1996.

Feherty is very curious and very open to learning. He got that wild-eyed look of his when I suggested that he try the belly button drill. A lot of golfers have a posture problem— when they take the club back, the upper part of their body tends to dip and the head goes down, and in the forward swing, everything comes up.

You'd like your upper torso to remain stable. Most teachers have you reference your head and have you hold it high. But when a tree falls, it really falls at the trunk and the roots. If the top of the tree falls, you can cut it off at the trunk.

The same holds true with the golfer. With a stable foundation, the head remains stable as well. That's why I talk about the navel. I ask players as they make their swing to hold the belly button up. In that way, you allow the upper body to remain erect.

My Foundation

I HAD LOVING, SUPPORTIVE PARENTS WHO GAVE ME EVERYTHING I needed and most of what I wanted. Dad, Edward Dominic Merrins, was a New Yorker sent to Meridian by his company, the Biddle Purchasing Company, to open an office there in 1929. Dad was a lumber broker and bought and sold lumber for his firm, which wasn't an easy proposition because he had come to Meridian at the cusp of the Great Depression. Meridian wasn't the wealthiest or the most prosperous place in the world, and business was difficult at best.

Dad met my mother, Carrie Lee Hand, a native of Meridian, and they married in 1931. A year later, I came along, christened Martin Edward Merrins, but I became known to all as "Little Eddie." Two years later, my sister, Marilyn, was born.

Dad's parents had immigrated to America from Ireland. He was raised in the Irish Catholic church and my mother was Southern Baptist, which was not an entirely easy combination in the South of the 1930s. When it came time to christen me, it caused a bit of a rift in our home. There was a certain stigma against Catholics in northern Mississippi, and my mother didn't understand Catholics. We were essentially raised in the Baptist church.

We went to church and Sunday school every Sunday. But I never set foot in that Catholic church, which was a half block away from the Baptist church where I was baptized. Our town's visiting Catholic priest was a man by the name of

Father Len Scannell from the Boston area. He was a career military man and he had been assigned to the military base in Meridian. He also was a golfer. If he hadn't become a priest, he probably would have been a golf professional. He was a good player and he took a liking to me.

I met him shortly after I began playing. He moved to different stations—Alaska, the Far East, and Houston—before he finally retired. All along, he stayed in touch with me, sending me letters along with the occasional phone call. He knew that by all rights I should have been raised in the Catholic church. So when I did convert to Catholicism at age thirty, he couldn't have been happier. He actually baptized our second son, Mason, in 1964.

Along the way I was influenced by a number of people who led to that decision on my part: Jay and Lionel Hebert, Dave Marr, Claude Harmon, Johnny Pott, and Tommy Jacobs. The common thread there, the link that influenced me, was their Catholic faith. Their living examples of their faith caused me to make the decision that allowed me to come to terms with my own faith. All the while Father Scannell was praying on my behalf, so I'm sure he had a lot of influence.

My parents believed in the value of education, especially because neither of them advanced beyond high school. They were insistent that Marilyn and I go on to college and saw to it that we received every opportunity. They gave us wonderful encouragement, made sure that we kept up with our studies, and took the necessary steps to see that we qualified to advance to college.

Dad was a five-day-a-week man at the brokerage office,

and at one point during the World War II years, he took over a lumber mill in Meridian and ran that for six largely unfruitful years. He gave it up in 1949 and returned to the brokerage business.

I could have learned the value of hard work from my parents, since they were both extremely hard workers. But my father didn't insist that I work to contribute to the well-being of the household or even earn my own spending money, such as having a newspaper route or cutting the neighborhood lawns. My parents were supportive of my golf. Dad never played golf, but he encouraged me and gave me the opportunity to play, for which I will always be grateful. I substituted hard work in the world with hard work on the course. As it turns out, that decision on all our parts served me in good stead for most of my lifetime.

Fortunately, I was able partly to repay their generosity by earning a golf scholarship to LSU. The scholarship helped pay off the investment they had made in me with their encouragement and the fact they sacrificed to finance my tournament play in the summertime. The full scholarship was the best present I could have given them at the time.

They were always there when my sister and I needed them, and I think that's the thing I admire the most. My mother did, however, want me to take piano lessons and dance lessons, which I avoided like the plague. In retrospect, she was right. I'd like to be able to play the piano and I'd like to be a better dancer.

Jason Gore

NO DOUBT, IF YOU WATCHED THE 2005 U.S. OPEN AT PINEHURST,
you know a bit of the story of Jason Gore. He became the
darling of the North Carolina fans, and the cheers for him
were the loudest on the course. Unfortunately, after being in
second place after three rounds, he shot a disappointing 84
in the final round, playing in the final pairing with third-
round leader Retief Goosen. A tournament that could have
meant his PGA Tour card and financial security turned into a
small check and cold reality.

That was the second time this young man learned the
value of winning by losing. You'll see what I mean.

I worked with Jason Gore for three years when he was a
product of our Southern California junior system. He attended Arizona and was a teammate of Jim Furyk and David
Berganio, which made for a terrific team. Jason won the
Pac-10 individual title as a freshman, and a wonderful college career lay ahead.

After some personal difficulty, he transferred to Pepper-
dine, and in his senior year, he and his team were poised to
win the NCAA Championship. Jason was in the last group
on the last day, and the team was almost assured of winning
the team title. He stood on the par-5 eighteenth tee needing
only a 5 to win individual honors.

He hit his tee shot into a fairway bunker, laid up with a
7-iron, and had still another 7-iron to the green. He then
made the mistake of his life. Jason pulled his third shot left of

the green into a deep bunker, with virtually no chance to get it up and down. He ended up making a 7 and lost the title.

Naturally, Jason was crestfallen. You don't get too many chances to win a national championship. I got a call from him the next week. He wanted to come see me and talk about the experience of his tragic final hole and what he might do to turn that around psychologically so that a negative could be transformed into a positive.

It was a very unusual approach for one so young. Most young people I know in that situation would simply repair to the practice tee, hit balls, lament, and make excuses. Not Jason.

We stood on the practice tee at Bel-Air and talked about his situation for about an hour and a half. He didn't hit a single ball the whole time. Over the next five weeks, he won the California State Amateur and the California Open. In the meantime, he was selected to the U.S. Walker Cup team.

Not many players have the strength of character to rebound like that.

The most important thing to know during a critical shot is that whatever your preshot routine is, don't deviate from it. Most bad shots at critical times come from the inability to remain positive over the shot. You can measure that expression the same way you measure strength. You know if you have given something 100 percent of your strength. You also know if you were 100 percent positive over a golf shot. You might not ever get to 100 percent, but treat it as the ideal.

Jason's story has a happy ending. After the debacle at the U.S. Open, he returned to the Nationwide Tour and won three straight tournaments, earning a "battlefield promotion" and immediate status on the PGA Tour. In only his second event on Tour after his promotion, he won the 84 Lumber Classic, thereby earning his playing privileges and a two-year exemption. And he did so by 2-putting for par from about 90 feet on the final hole to win by a shot.

Not only did he learn from tragedy, as it turns out, he profited from it.

Brotherly Love

ONE NEVER KNOWS WHERE HELP IS GOING TO COME FROM WHEN you need it most. In 1962, I was an assistant pro at Westchester Country Club in New York and was trying to make a living playing the Tour. The opportunity came along to become head professional at Bel-Air. I was playing a practice round at a Tour event with Jay Hebert and gave him the news that day. In those days, most pros didn't receive a salary. They earned a living from selling merchandise from the pro shop and from the lessons they gave. Stocking the pro shop came from the pro's pocket, and a new pro could have some trouble getting started if he was short on funds.

After our practice round, in the locker room, Jay slipped a piece of paper in my pocket. I looked later to discover a check for $10,000. The accompanying note merely said, "You're going to need this to open your golf shop at Bel-Air." He gave me this money, quite a sum at the time, with no strings attached. He just wanted me to do well.

How many golf pros would do such a thing? Jay and his brother Lionel were perhaps the greatest brother act ever to play professional golf, and it's a real shame that more people don't know about the Hebert brothers. In fact, they were probably the most underrated pair of brothers in all of golf. Lionel won the 1957 PGA Championship, the last championship to be contended at match play, and Jay won the 1959 PGA Championship. Lionel was a fabulous entertainer and loved to play his trumpet. All it took was a call and Lionel would jump into the band and play at the slightest provocation.

But it was their spirit of giving that made them stand out among their peers. They helped any number of young, aspiring pros who needed support. I was fortunate to be on the receiving end.

The Lesson Begins

I START EVERY LESSON BY ASKING MY STUDENT what he wants to do. I want him to be somewhat in command. I'm the teacher, it's my little office, and I'm in charge of that office, but I want him to be a part. It's the essence of two-way communication.

So I need to know what's going through a student's mind to see what he really wants. I can see what he's doing—or attempting to do—but I need to know what he wants to achieve. That's how I try to tailor the instruction. What I teach, I teach everybody, but it's like I've got a pharmacy filled with concoctions and you're the patient. You don't need the whole pharmacy; you need whatever remedy suits your ills.

Each student is unique in that he's at a different stage in the learning process, and at that very stage, he needs to confess what's on his mind. Like in my own case, if I were seeking an instructor, and I'm going to expose myself to some teacher, I'm going to find out why I'm not making proper contact. I know what I'm trying to do, and I know in my own mind what I think is right, but there is something getting in the way there. Until I clear that up, I'm not going to be playing the kind of golf I feel I can play. So if I went to a teacher, I'd communicate that with him. That's what I want to know.

I don't want to know everything the teacher knows. I want the answer to my question. I want a student to communicate that to me. I want to address whatever question he has in mind and I'll try to answer that satisfactorily. Usually that satisfaction leads to another question. One question leads to another.

Ultimately, the answer to whatever question the student has comes down to Swing the Handle. That's where the concept of the swing starts and ends.

Dean Martin

ONE OF MY PRIZED POSSESSIONS IS A PHOTOGRAPH OF BEN HOGAN, shot from behind on his follow-through during his 1950 U.S. Open victory at Merion, where I served as an assistant professional. That photo hung above the door to my office at Bel-Air for a number of years.

One of my other prized possessions is a photograph of Dean Martin, in the Hogan pose, signed by Martin and dedicated to me. It hung beside the photo of Hogan in my office, in no less a revered spot.

Dean Martin was one of the most popular members that Bel-Air ever had. He was just so entertaining to be around. He was funny, he was witty, he was charming, and he loved the club. His reputation was that of a drinker, but he hardly drank when he was at Bel-Air.

His routine was to turn up at the club around 11:30 A.M., hit a few balls, and have some lunch. His regular group—some three foursomes—would gather at about 12:30 and the choosing of teams would take place. Every permutation of partners would be booked with bets, and the group needed a bookkeeper to keep track of all the action.

They weren't playing for an insignificant amount of money, of which Martin had plenty and everyone knew it. Every player in that gangsome was trying to get into Martin's pocket and he loved it. Trouble was, he never played well enough to return the favor and separate his opponents from some of their money. He came in on the losing end more often than not, which always made him welcome anytime in the lunchtime game.

Special Interest

OF ALL THE PEOPLE AT NORTHWOOD COUNTRY CLUB IN MERIDIAN who took an interest in me, a couple of them stand out. One was Hunter George Weddington. He won the Mississippi State Amateur twice and was quite an outstanding player. But he was equally outstanding as a person.

He spent a lot of time with me when I was growing up, playing with me when he could have been spending his time elsewhere. We'd play for quarters and 50-cent pieces. Not only did I have the experience of playing with someone who was better than I was, he seemed to be genuinely concerned for my welfare, both as a golf player and as a young person.

He was good, and he needled me to no end. That was a great favor he did for me because it helped drive me to get better. He also took me to tournaments that we'd enter. He'd be driving, chatting away with his wife while smoking that big cigar he always seemed to have in his mouth. I'd be in the backseat, most likely asleep, waiting to get wherever we were going.

Another prominent influence on my young golf life was Gene Vinson, who five times won the Mississippi State Amateur. He could take his game nationally, too, having played into the fifth round of the U.S. Amateur on one occasion. When I was seventeen, Gene took me to the Southern Amateur in New Orleans. He was a colonel in the Air National Guard and had access to the Guard airplanes. He commandeered a B-26 and off we went to New Orleans. You couldn't do that today, and I'm not so certain he didn't get away with something then. But it certainly was a thrill for someone so young.

Once in 1949, I was playing in a sixsome on a Wednesday afternoon at Northwood and made two holes in one: on the thirteenth hole and on the seventeenth. In that sixsome, there was a man by the name of T. Miller. Miller was a federal marshal, so when all the commotion occurred and these two holes in one were recorded—it actually went into *Ripley's Believe It or Not*—he said, "Don't mention my name as having played." He didn't want the taxpayers to see he'd been out playing golf on a Wednesday afternoon when he was supposed to be working.

The club had one of those rules that if you made a hole in one, you had to buy drinks for everybody. So my father was summoned to come and bail me out. He had to help with the bar tab for all those guys.

I matured quickly under this intense golf education. Playing with older people makes you handle yourself better because more is expected of you. And it certainly made me play better golf more quickly because I was up against some stiff competition, not only from Northwood members who were better than I was but also against some of the members who were state- and national-caliber players.

Plus, I had been raised on a tight, hilly, tree-lined golf course. Out of necessity, I had to learn to hit the ball straight. As a result, tight fairways never bothered me. I felt comfortable because it looked like home to me. And I had become accustomed to shooting 65s and 66s, so later on, when I was in a position to produce a low score, I knew how. It's not as if I had never done it before. If you aren't comfortable with low scores, if they scare you, you'll never shoot them on a regular basis. If you are a 3-under-par player, you need to think about going 4 under. Every time you have a low score working, think about making it even lower. I learned that playing with the good players at Northwood.

That same year, when I was seventeen, I played an exhibition match with the great Sam Snead. He had just shot 63-63 over the final two rounds to win the Texas Open, and he drove from San Antonio to Meridian for this Tuesday exhibition. Snead and I were teamed together, and we played Vinson and Weddington. We nipped them 1-up. It was a nice match, but what made it even nicer was that I shot 68, which was the low score of the foursome. Snead shot 71.

But, as was the case when I scored lower than Byron Nelson in an exhibition later that summer, I had no illusions of grandeur.

Ben Hogan

GREATNESS IS SOMETIMES ENCOUNTERED IN THE MOST UNLIKELY OF places. At the 1957 U.S. Open, I found myself in the players' locker room at the adjoining urinal next to the great Ben Hogan.

I said to myself, "This is hardly the place to encounter an immortal!"

During my tenure at Merion Golf Club (1957–59), I was drawn into the "Hogan mystique" by the legend surrounding his 1950 U.S. Open victory there. Francis Sullivan, a Merion member, was Hogan's personal and legal counsel and one of his very best friends. Sullivan became like a surrogate father to me and served as godfather to my son Michael. Through this relationship, Ben provided me a set of clubs (1959 model), which were duplicates of his personal clubs. I played with that set of irons for twenty-five years.

On my journey from New York (the Rockaway Hunting Club and Westchester Country Club) to Bel-Air to become head professional there in 1962, Frank Sullivan arranged for me to stop by Fort Worth and visit the Ben Hogan Golf Company. Ben and his wife, Valerie, could not have been more accommodating. "A friend of Francis Sullivan is a friend of ours," they exclaimed. It was no accident that Hogan equipment had a prominent place in the Bel-Air golf shop for a number of years.

We renewed our acquaintance during the 1966 U.S. Open at Olympic, where Bob Goalby, Ed Tutweiler, and I were paired just in front of Hogan, Ken Venturi, and Frank Beard. We were swarmed over by their gallery, but the experience was great. Out of retirement by special invitation from the USGA, Hogan excited everyone with his play.

In the mid-1980s, Bel-Air member and former football

Eddie Merrins

great Tom Harmon had Ben as a guest. He set me straight regarding the photograph of him that hung over the door to my office, which pictured him playing to the eighteenth green at Merion during the 1950 U.S. Open. It was not the picture of him playing the famous 1-iron shot that got him into a tie with Lloyd Mangrum and George Fazio. Rather, it was almost a duplicate from the same line to the green (featuring a different outfit) but nearer the green from where he played a 5-iron shot to clinch victory in the eighteen-hole playoff.

The Harmon-Hogan relationship led to the creation of the Ben Hogan Trophy, which was established in 1988 to honor the male college golfer of the year. It has become the Heisman Trophy of college golf. I enjoyed the privilege of presenting Ben a replica of this Waterford Crystal trophy that is on display at Bel-Air at a presentation in his Fort Worth office arranged by mutual friend Rayburn Tucker of Dallas. This creation is a product of our Friends of Golf organization. Tom Harmon, the 1940 Heisman Trophy winner, was proudly a director of FOG and solely responsible for Ben Hogan lending his name to this award.

The replica stood front and center in the Hogan Room display at Colonial Country Club. It now sits with the rest of his trophies and medals in the Ben Hogan Room at Golf House, the USGA home in New Jersey.

Death took Hogan from us in 1997, but his impression on the golfing world is indelible. Likely the greatest ball striker of all time, his style and example were copied by many. His manner was to keep close to the vest with everything near.

He had legions of admirers but only a few confidants. Those people were treated to a rare individual.

Hogan's funeral service at the TCU Methodist Church in Fort Worth was typical of his life: plain, simple, to the point, no eulogies, and without fanfare. Only two stands of white carnations served as decorations. Ben must have enjoyed the last scene, which featured Sam Snead and Tommy Bolt in their black suits walking side by side down the aisle, as two of his pallbearers. Surely he was delighted.

Hands On

YOUR HANDS ARE YOUR ONLY CONNECTION TO the handle of the club, so you'd best make certain they are on the handle the right way. And the only right way that I know of for the hands to be is on the side of the shaft. What I mean by that is you don't want to put your left hand on top of the

shaft and your right hand underneath in the so-called hook position. Nor do you want your left hand underneath and your right hand on top in the so-called slice position.

It's much easier to see the relation between the hands and clubface when you hold the club in the middle of the shaft. Each hand should be in line squarely with the face of the club. The palm of your right hand and the score lines of the club are in the same direction. The same goes for the back of your left hand. With your hands to the side of the shaft, it's only natural that they are in line with the clubface.

And take your grip with the club in the air. If you set your hands with the club on the ground, you tend to make wrong adjustments and change things. It's much easier to get the relationship you want with the club in the air. You wouldn't take your grip on a tennis racket with the racket lying on the ground. Neither should you do so with a golf club.

College Education

ON THE STRENGTH OF WINNING THE MISSISSIPPI STATE AMATEUR and the Jaycee National Junior, I was offered a full scholarship at Louisiana State. In 1950, scholarships for golf were not very prevalent. Because of the school's steeped reputation in golf that dated back to the middle 1930s, LSU was one of the few schools at that time that did award scholarships.

Freddie Haas played there in the '30s; Dale Morey and NCAA champion Earl Stewart were there in the '40s, along with Gardner Dickinson, Jay Hebert, Joe Moore Jr., Jack Coyle, Sonny Ellis, and Jim Ryan. Most of those guys had been in the service during World War II and had come back to complete their education. I was impressed with that, so I chose LSU instead of Ole Miss, where my sister went to school.

I had the opportunity during those years to play a lot of

high-level, national-caliber golf, both in college and in major amateur events. I competed in the NCAA Championship for three years—freshmen couldn't play in those days, and they didn't have the rule that's in place today where players can take five years to complete four years' eligibility.

I did have my successes in college. I won the Southeastern Conference championship twice, in 1953 and 1954. I also won the Southern Intercollegiate in 1953. And, as a sopho-more in 1952, I went to the finals of the NCAA Champi-onship—the individual title was played at match play in those years. I lost 1-down to Jimmy Vickers of Oklahoma in the final match at Purdue. Over the thirty-six holes, neither player was ever more than 1-up. Vickers rolled in a 30-footer for birdie on the final hole to win the match. We both sat down and had a nice cry over it.

As a senior in 1954, at Brae Burn in Houston, I advanced to the semifinals, losing to my LSU teammate, Cecil Cal-houn. Cecil, in turn, lost to Hillman Robbins of Memphis State in the final match. As a team, we almost won the cham-pionship in 1953 at the Broadmoor in Colorado Springs. I was the fourth low qualifier, having shot 75-66, the 66 hav-ing tied the competitive course record at the time.

We made quite a comeback after shooting a four-man team total of 308 on the first day. The same four players on the same golf course shot 273, and we made up 30 shots on Texas, which was leading the event. In fact, we finished 6 shots ahead of Texas. But we had Stanford to deal with. There was one player on the course who could knock us out. Grant Spaeth shot 32 on the back nine, and Stanford beat us by 3 shots. Spaeth would become the president of the USGA some forty years later.

In the summertime, I played as much national-level amateur golf as I could. In 1951, at age eighteen, I went to the finals of the Southern Amateur, losing to Arnold Blum. I would have been the youngest player to win the Southern since Bobby Jones did it in 1917 at age fifteen. I qualified for the U.S. Amateur four straight years, from 1952 to 1955, and in 1954 at the Country Club of Detroit, I made it to the fifth round. In those days, if you won your fifth-round match, you advanced to the quarterfinals, which earned you an invitation to the Masters. My trip to Augusta was derailed by Bob Sweeney, who eventually lost to Arnold Palmer in the finals.

My crowning achievement as an amateur was at the 1955 Western Amateur at Rockford, Illinois. I beat Hillman Robbins in the final on the thirty-seventh hole to win the title. It was a huge victory because the Western was second in importance on the amateur landscape to the U.S. Amateur. It gave me a ten-year exemption into the Western Open, one that I would use long into my professional career.

Arnold Palmer

LONG BEFORE HE BECAME FAMOUS FOR HIS NOW LEGENDARY charges to victory, I was the victim of an Arnold Palmer onslaught. In 1954, I was leading the All-American Amateur

Championships at Tam O'Shanter in Chicago by 1 shot with ten holes to play in the final round.

I played the next seven holes in 1 under par and still lost 6 strokes to Palmer. He played that stretch in 7 under, with two pars, two eagles, and three birdies. He went on to win by 7 and I finished second, wondering what had just happened.

I first became acquainted with Palmer in 1950 at the now extinct Tennessee Valley Invitational in Chattanooga, a wonderful tournament that featured such great players as Harvie Ward, Gay Brewer, Gardner Dickinson, Lew Oehmig, Hillman Robbins, Mason Rudolph, Fred Wampler, Hobart Manley, and many others of the nation's top amateurs.

A few years later, when Arnold was out of the Coast Guard and attending Wake Forest, he played in the 1954 Southern Intercollegiate in Athens, Georgia. He and I finished second and third, respectively, behind Robbins's final-round 66.

In those days, a slick entrepreneur named George S. May conducted two weeks of tournaments in Chicago. The first week was the All-American, in which pros and amateurs competed in two separate but simultaneous events. The next week was the World Championships, in much the same fashion. The week after Palmer won the All-American Amateur, he won the amateur division of the World Championship. Frank Stranahan was second and I was third.

Had he won the pro division, he would have taken home $50,000 and another $50,000 in guaranteed exhibitions. It was an enormous sum for that time.

I had just witnessed, close up, the arrival of Arnold

Palmer. In a one-month period, he won the All-American, the World Championship, and the U.S. Amateur title. It was a portent of things to come when he decided to leave his sales job in Cleveland (working for Pine Valley member Bill Wehnes) to turn pro. Arnie's Army was being formed, and Mark McCormack was beginning to realize a dream for Palmer and himself.

As fate would have it, some forty-eight years later, as Arnold was rehearsing for the Masters on a Wednesday in 2002, the Little Pro was visiting with the King on the practice tee in Augusta. Arnold lamented that his golf swing felt short and tight. I suggested to him that I was confident I could correct his problem. Lo and behold, the next day he shot 89, his worst ever Masters score! At his postround interview he pronounced that enough was enough and the next day he played what we thought would be his last Masters round. (Turns out, he waited until 2004 to officially say good-bye.) Arnold did not blame my Wednesday instruction for his demise on Thursday, being the gracious performer he is. Isn't it ironic that almost fifty years later, my well-intentioned suggestions lent to a payback of sorts for the lessons he had given me in 1954.

Palmer has been perhaps the most accommodating public figure I have ever had the pleasure of knowing. I marveled at how he handled the autograph seekers and well-wishers. His patience and graciousness were a model to be admired.

At a black-tie dinner in Los Angeles, Pat Reilly, then president of the PGA of America, Paul Runyan, and I were asked to present Palmer as Man of the Year for the Jonathan Club.

In my presentation I told the gathering about Arnold being the most accommodating public figure I had ever encountered and suggested, "It is good that Arnie hadn't been born a girl because he never knew how to say no!"

Set Yourself Free

IF YOUR GOLF SWING FEELS TOO TENSE AND tight, take time to free your joints. Your body has an extensive system of joints and muscles. The muscles act like a series of rubber bands stretching and giving. However, the joints must be perfectly free in order for the body to respond. This is certainly the case within your golf swing.  Differentiate between the joints and muscles. The joints should be free (not tense and locked) but the muscles are in use (active).

To create a longer swing, mentally focus on the hub of the club (opposite from the clubhead) and physically make as big a swing as you feel like. You do not lengthen your swing at the clubhead; you do so at the hub. This was my lesson to Arnold Palmer.

Harvey Penick

PERHAPS NO OTHER TEACHER, THROUGH HIS WRITINGS AND HIS
students, is more beloved than Harvey Penick. His *Little
Red Book* and the subsequent volumes introduced the
world to a man who devoted his life to teaching golf to
the rank-and-file handicap player who is the backbone of
our game.

He was best known for developing Ben Crenshaw and
Tom Kite as juniors at Austin Country Club in the Texas cap-
ital. He also had a big hand in the development of LPGA
stars Betsy Rawls and Mickey Wright.

When Bud Shrake, who helped Harvey write the *Little*
books, told him that his portion of the book's advance would
be $40,000, Harvey paused for a long moment.

"Bud, I don't know where I'm going to get $40,000," said
Harvey, thinking he was going to have to pay to have the
book published rather than the other way around.

When I was coaching at UCLA in the late 1970s, I had a
young student, Fred Warren, who wanted to learn from the
best. I called Harvey and he took Fred under his wing, and
with the help of Labron Harris at Oklahoma State, Fred became one of the country's top golf coaches.

The 1995 Masters was a true celebration of Harvey's life
and death. Student Davis Love III won the week before the
Masters at New Orleans, a victory that put him into the
Masters. Word was passed to Harvey on his sickbed, and he
smiled. Later that evening he died.

Kite and Crenshaw commandeered a private jet and flew back to Austin for the funeral. Love desperately wanted to go along, but Kite and Crenshaw convinced him to stay and prepare for the Masters.

As it turned out, it was Crenshaw who won the Masters, as a special tribute to Penick. "I had a fifteenth club in my bag today," Ben said. "It was Harvey."

Testing the Water

IF YOU WANT TO BECOME A COMPETITIVE TOUR-nament player, you should play against the best players you can find—at your level. That sometimes means playing with older players, more mature players, and players who are just plain better than you are. For juniors that means stepping out

and playing against the older players at your course or club, or playing in the state junior or even a national junior event.

You must subject yourself to the highest possible competitive environment you can reach so that if you eventually find yourself in that arena, anything equal to or below that level will be especially comfortable to you. If you've played in the state amateur, the city amateur and the club championship won't look so intimidating. Similarly, if you're good enough to qualify for the U.S. Amateur, you should be especially confident to play in the state amateur. The point is that you have to be willing to stretch yourself. If you do, your comfort level will increase in every tournament you play, no matter the scale.

You must want to raise the bar. But you can't go from one level to a level ten steps above. That's too much of a quantum leap. It has to be step by step. I followed that progression through the junior ranks, from the club junior to the national junior. The one thing I didn't do was to qualify for the U.S. Open. I attempted qualifying only once and didn't play in the Open until 1957 when I turned pro. But I did play in the Baton Rouge Open and the All-American World Championship in Chicago.

All were good experiences and necessary to my progression as a golf player.

Putting

PUTTING IS SIMPLE: READ THE PUTT, ROLL THE ball, and think in terms of making it. All the great putters roll the ball instead of hitting it. And we roll the ball by moving the handle of the putter through the ball.

Many people focus on the putter head when putting, but if you do, the handle moves backward—and you don't want that in any shot you play. Begin by addressing an 8-foot putt and roll the ball into the hole without taking a backswing, moving the handle of the putter through the ball. Now take a backswing but concentrate on rolling the ball using the handle of the putter.

So your mental approach is to make every putt from the 2-inch backhand to the 100-footer. You try to make every putt.

As ten-year-old caddie Eddie Lowery told twenty-year-old Francis Ouimet as he battled Vardon and Ray at Brookline in 1913 (as quoted in the film *The Greatest Game Ever Played*), "Francis, in putting you read it, roll it, and hole it."

John Wooden

JOHN WOODEN IS ONE OF THE GREATEST MEN I HAVE EVER KNOWN. I had the exceptional opportunity to become acquainted with him in 1975 when I began coaching at UCLA and he was in the last year of his storied basketball coaching tenure. We went around the track together in the stadium; he had a heart condition and walked five miles daily and I was into jogging at the time. Truth is, he could walk as fast as I could jog.

Much of our time together, we talked golf. He liked to talk about Byron Nelson quite a bit. They weren't friends, they didn't even know each other to my knowledge. But they were great kindred spirits. Both were among the greatest of their profession. Both held the highest ideals. Both were gentlemen and gentle men.

Wooden represents the best of college athletics—the opportunity to play on the highest plane with the sole purpose of giving your very best. If you did that, he believed, winning might come your way. But he never looked at winning as the end-all goal. With Wooden, it was all about preparation. Be properly prepared and the rewards will come.

I asked him to address the golf team at UCLA on one occasion. I asked him to speak about winning, figuring no one else was better suited to talk about that topic. We had a joint meeting of the men's and women's golf teams and I even invited some Bel-Air members to attend.

He prepared like a college lecturer and spoke for an hour and twenty minutes. Never once did he mention the word *winning*. He always talked about preparation. If you ever had the opportunity to see one of his teams perform, they almost never showed up to play unprepared. They didn't win every time—most of the time, mind you—but they were always ready to play.

He knew how to cajole and he knew how to administer discipline if need be. The biggest case in point is how he dealt with Bill Walton during his rebel years at UCLA. Walton, to this day, considers John Wooden maybe his best friend. Hardly a day goes by that he doesn't give his coach a telephone call.

In 1974, UCLA was the defending NCAA champion, having won the previous seven titles in a row, unheard-of then and absolutely unheard-of now. That year, the Bruins lost an eight-point lead in overtime against N.C. State and David Thompson in the NCAA semifinals, breaking the streak. To this day, Walton heaps total blame on himself for losing that game. That's what his coach means to him.

UCLA won the national championship again in 1975,

beating Kentucky in the final game, and shortly afterward, Wooden announced his retirement.

I'd say in his ninety-fifth year, he's as alert and bright as he ever was. His physical condition is not what it once was; he's suffered. But through it all, he's been the absolute model to compare to in every way—as a human being, a coach, an athlete, and a friend to hundreds of students to whom he has lent his guidance.

Most people don't know that Coach Wooden loves poetry and is always touched when someone sends him a poem.

We had an event at Bel-Air that Al Michaels emceed, at which Wooden was the guest of honor. After their interview, which was classic, the floor opened for questions from the audience and one came Wooden's way.

"Coach, what do you do to motivate your players?" he was asked.

He thought for a second and said, "I pat them on the head." He let a little time elapse and he said, "Or maybe a little lower down."

Equal but Opposite

WHEN SETTING YOUR HANDS ON THE CLUB, you should have an equal but opposite grip pressure. What I mean by that is the pressure your hands exert will work in opposite directions.

Your fingers wrap around the club so they lock the handle of the club under the heel of each hand. I don't subscribe to the notion of holding tighter in one hand than you do in the other. That makes for an imbalance in the grip. Instead, it's as though the fingers of your right hand want to turn the club to the right and the fingers of your left hand want to turn the club to the left. In this way, you have offsetting pressure. The golf grip is a two-sided affair, as is the swing.

In order to fit your hands so they don't work apart, set each thumb on the opposite side of the shaft. Your left thumb fits slightly on the right side of the shaft and your right thumb does the opposite. In this way, your hands remarkably fit each other. The pressure is still in the fingers. If you tighten your fingers, your hands will actually wrench off the club. And the thumb of your left hand fits nicely in the pocket formed by the palm of your right hand. It's a hand-in-glove fit.

Mental Makeup

ATTITUDE IS EVERYTHING IN THE MAKEUP OF A golfer. In my career, I have seen players with attitudes at both extremes and everything in between. The player who possesses a good attitude does not react to the outcome of a shot. A single shot, good or

bad, does not at all affect the golf player with a good attitude.

On the other hand, those with a bad attitude allow the result of the shot to affect not only who they are as a golfer but also who they are as a person. No group of people beat up on themselves any worse than golfers do. If you could play back the things you've said to yourself on the golf course, you'd be appalled. You are supposed to be your own best friend, but you wouldn't treat your best friend that way, would you?

We talk about players developing an even-keel attitude. We know the consequences of becoming too exhilarated over a good shot and too despondent over a bad one. It's easy to talk about, and if we could buy some of that attitude at the store, we'd all be better off. Learning to keep our emotions level is a constant struggle.

In the end, the battle is always against Old Man Par. If we start playing well and get 2 or 3 under par, we remember that someone somewhere is 10 under par at that moment. If you hit a lousy shot, so what? If you hit a great shot, so what? Why hamstring yourself psychologically?

The mental aspect can actually make a winner out of an ordinary player. We like to be around people and players who are positive. Gary Player comes to mind as someone who is always positive. Tiger Woods is the example we look to today. His attitude is exemplary and getting even better.

Let's suppose you are playing a golf shot and you find your ball in the rough grass, or even in the forest, and you have a small gap in the trees and have to carry the water onto the green. What do you do? You take a number of negative possibilities and change that into a positive by choosing a conservative route back to the fairway and then onto the green. By acting conservatively and learning the art of sacrifice, you may sacrifice part of a shot, but you don't sacrifice the whole shot.

In every situation, you should be looking for the positive that offsets the negative. For instance, I don't know a player who stands on the first tee who is not anxious and nervous. Stand there and toss a ball in the air and catch it. Whether you know it or not, you are practicing hypnosis. You are focused on the ball in the simple act of tossing and catching, and you become relaxed and very confident that you are going to complete the task with no effort whatsoever. You can tune out the rest of the world by focusing on the ball. Hypnosis is a form of relaxation.

The conscious being is put to rest and the subconscious takes over with the act of tossing and catching the ball. The trick is to transfer that to the ball you play golf with, so that when you look at the golf ball, your body goes into a relaxed state and you swing subconsciously. That's where you perform your best.

Your best mental makeup can be described with the four P's. Remain positive at all times. Be patient when it looks as if you need to make up a lot of ground in a short period of time. Be persistent and stay in your routine and control the things you can control. And above all, have perseverance and never give up or give in.

Physical Makeup

IT'S WELL-KNOWN THAT MANY OF THE TOP PRO-
fessionals take part in strenuous physical
workouts in order to enhance their ability
to swing the club more efficiently and ath-
letically. Most of us don't go to that extreme. However, there are some physical
things you should be doing, especially be-

fore the round, to make your golf swing work a little better.

Take the club in hand, lift the club over your head, and
arch your back. That lengthens your spine and stretches your
back. Now take the club in both hands and bend over as if
you were going to touch your toes. Bend your knees a little
and you should feel the stretch in your lower back and the
backs of your legs.

Now, the split-hand drill: With your hands split apart on
the handle, take the club back as far as you can, and you
should feel the stretch along your whole left side. Now swing
the club slowly to the left side, and you should feel the stretch
along your right side.

In the Bench stretch, as in Johnny Bench, you take the club
on each end in both hands and raise it over your head, bend-
ing toward the ground on one side of the body as far as you
can. You will feel the stretching take place in the left side lower
body and right side upper body. Then go to the other side.

Do these things before you hit a shot, and your muscles

will thank you. Exercise for golfers should be four-part: cardio, flexibility, strength-building, swing-building.

Measuring Up

I THINK I'VE ALWAYS HAD A BIT OF AN INFERIORITY COMPLEX. I gave people I was playing against as much respect as they were entitled to, maybe even more. I expected that players would be better than perhaps they were, and it always left me wondering if I could measure up.

From the time I was fourteen, part of me thought I could stand up to better players, but another part thought that might not be the case. I started competing locally, then regionally, and then nationally. I had success at all levels, even winning the Jaycee National Juniors at age seventeen. But it wasn't until I accepted the scholarship to LSU that I really had the feeling that I needed to prove my worth. The university was investing a lot of money in me and my golf ability, and I wanted to show that the investment was worthwhile. When it was all said and done, after my college career was completed, I felt very satisfied that I had done enough to justify that scholarship.

In college, when we practiced or played for fun, I always had the feeling that I wasn't playing up to my potential. I played as well as I could, in the company of my college teammates, but I always thought it could be better. In competition, on the other hand, I seemed to play better than my teammates and even my competitors. I seemed to play under my head for fun and over my head for keeps. I think that the feeling of not measuring up to the others helped drive me in that way. The fear of failure is, and was, a great motivating factor.

I think that's what drove Ben Hogan. He had a meager background and a limited education. He grew up in the shadow of Byron Nelson—they both caddied at Glen Garden Country Club in Fort Worth—and wasn't nearly as successful early in his career as he was later. He felt that he had a lot to prove and continued to feel that way until the end of his career and even his life.

That's why he was such a perfectionist. It's also why he was so closed about inviting people into his inner circle and equally reticent about giving of himself. He was a very private man who was one of the greatest players of all time and who became a very successful businessman. He accumulated wealth and prestige, and I think that brought him a certain satisfaction.

I believe that Vijay Singh is somewhat like Hogan in that regard. Singh is driven internally by, if not a feeling of inferiority, something akin to that. The only way he can prove himself a great player is to shut himself off from the world, keep his inner circle small, and work as hard as he can as long as he can. He spends most of his waking hours hitting balls on the range in a constant effort to become even better. That hard work gives him his confidence, the inner peace that comes with knowing he is as prepared as anyone, better than most. It can't help but silence his critics, and his record speaks for itself.

I've always looked up to anyone who has achieved success in his or her field. Successful people are unusual in that they are not content to be one among many. They want to achieve a level above the rest. They cut themselves out of the herd and pursue goals and dreams with a vigor that others simply don't have. These people are exceptional, and I've always wanted to know what makes them that way.

I want to know what Vince Lombardi and John Wooden are all about. I want to know about Bart Starr and Joe Namath and what makes them tick. Having the opportunity that I've enjoyed at Bel-Air, I've been surrounded by successful people, whether they come from the field of athletics, entertainment, or business. It has been fascinating to learn about their makeup. The common denominators that I've seen are that they love competition and they all enjoy an opportunity to excel. And none of them is satisfied with second place.

Nor are they satisfied with mediocrity. Many people in this life do just enough to get by without ever tasting the sweet fruit of achievement. Whether we're talking about school or your job or your avocation, never be content with the ordinary. The people who succeed work constantly at getting better. Tiger Woods and Vijay Singh, the top two players in the world, as good as they are, never stop working. And if they don't win, they aren't satisfied.

Those are the real champions. Hogan was that way. Nicklaus, too. Jack Nicklaus didn't want to be almost as good as Bobby Jones. He wanted to be better. He wasn't content to live in the shadow of Arnold Palmer. He wanted to achieve more. He didn't think it enough to be mentioned in the same

breath as Ben Hogan. He wanted to win more major championships than anyone.

There is only one Nicklaus. Most of us will set our sights
much lower. But we all, in our own small ways, can be no less
determined to reach our goals.

Amateur Golf's Golden Age

IN THE 1950S, AMATEUR GOLF WAS BIGGER THAN THE PROFES-
sional game. That's hard to believe today, especially when we
talk about the purses of the PGA Tour and the prestige of
and interest in the major championships. Today, amateur
golf is little more than an afterthought on the game's landscape, a pleasant competitive diversion for part-time players.

However, in the Golden Age, amateurs ruled. I was fortunate enough to have played top-level amateur golf in the
1950s, and I witnessed some of the best golf I have ever seen.
I played in the U.S. Amateur only four times and I never
came close to winning. Messrs. Don Albert, Robert Kosten,
Bob Sweeney, and Fred Gordon all saw to it that my name
was not to grace the Havermeyer Trophy. God bless them:
Unbeknownst to me, they helped drive me into teaching.
However, I did win the Western Amateur in 1955, which, at
the time, was the second most prestigious tournament in
amateur golf. And it gave me a ten-year exemption into the
Western Open, a tournament once ranked with the professional majors in importance.

In the '50s, World War II was over, colleges were thriving and offering scholarships to golfers, and business catered to the amateurs, leaving the professionals to compete for meager purses and even more meager media attention. Bobby Jones, thirty years earlier, was the model to be emulated for golfers of skill. He was a gentleman golfer, working as a lawyer and educated as an engineer, playing our great game while still managing to work for a living. That was how golfers thought they should conduct their lives.

Some of the great amateurs of that era, who helped shape the game in that era:

- Frank Stranahan—Known as much for having substantial wealth and being a fitness fanatic as for his golf, Stranahan was one of the few Americans who won the British Amateur in the modern era. In fact, he was second to Ben Hogan at the 1953 British Open at Carnoustie, the year Hogan won three major championships. Stranahan was developed as a junior by his club pro, Byron Nelson, at Inverness.

- Billy Maxwell—The first of the outstanding college players of this era. Maxwell's North Texas State team won the NCAA Championships four consecutive years (1949–52). Not so coincidentally, North Texas State coach Fred Cobb employed the services of the great Byron Nelson to help coach the team. Maxwell went through eight matches in grand style to win the 1951 U.S. Amateur at Saucon Valley.

- Charlie Coe—Another of that group who rarely gets mentioned is Coe. It would be hard to find a player of that era who was better. He won the 1949 and the 1958 U.S. Amateur and finished second in 1959 to Jack Nicklaus in one of the greatest U.S. Amateur final matches of all time. And he finished second by a stroke to Gary Player in the 1961 Masters. He might be underrated and under-appreciated by the media, but he is held in high regard by those who know amateur golf. Charlie was in the oil business and lived most of his life in Oklahoma City. As it happened, the 1953 U.S. Amateur was held at Oklahoma City Golf and Country Club and Charlie drew Harvie Ward in the third round. They had a match that should have been reserved for a final match. Ward finally won after the match had gone five extra holes. That one was talked about for years.

- Arnold Palmer—Few talk about Arnold as a great amateur, but he had a record that was the envy of most. He won the George S. May All-American and World Championship in Chicago and steamrolled the field in the U.S. Amateur—all in the same year, 1954.

- E. Harvie Ward—One of the best amateurs of all time would have amassed an even more impressive record had Ward not lost his amateur status when the USGA determined that his employer, Ed Lowery, was paying his tournament expenses. Ward won the 1955 and 1956 U.S. Amateur but was denied a chance to make it three straight when the USGA made its ruling. He was not the same thereafter.

- Gene Littler—Perhaps the most overlooked player on the American scene was San Diego's Gene Littler. Dominating junior golf (winning the Jaycee National Junior), ruling amateur golf (winning the 1953 U.S. Amateur over Dale Morey and capturing the San Diego Open Tour event in 1954 as an amateur), excelling on the PGA Tour (winning more than thirty events, including the U.S. Open in 1961), and dominating the Senior Tour for fifteen years, Littler escapes the radar only because he prefers it that way. As an amateur, there was none better.

Three Choices

THERE ARE THREE TRADITIONAL GRIPS. THE most popular is the Vardon, where you lap the little finger of your right hand over the forefinger of your left. In the interlocking, favored by Jack Nicklaus and Tiger Woods, you interlock the little finger of your right hand with the forefinger of  your left. Or you can put all eight fingers on the club in the so-called baseball grip.

You have a choice and it doesn't matter which you subscribe to; it's a matter of what feels most comfortable to you. You can, if you want, spread the forefinger of each hand slightly away from the middle finger, creating a little space between them. In your right hand, it creates a trigger finger effect, and in your left, it makes a space to lap the little finger of your right hand.

If you really want to refine the grip, you can slightly pinch the thumb and forefinger together so that you raise the muscle in between. By so doing, when your club is at the end of the backswing, it creates a little cradle for your club to rest in.

Basic Training

I GRADUATED FROM SCHOOL IN 1955, AND AS A RESULT OF THE ROTC program at LSU, I had a commission in the Air Force. I got out of the service early because I had a medical discharge, and I took a job working for an automobile agency in Meridian selling Buicks for a man by the name of C. W. Fewell. That was a favorite job of amateur golfers at that time because it gave you an opportunity to make a little money but it also gave you an opportunity to play your golf, and one kind of complemented the other. That was the thing that amateurs did in that day.

If they were fortunate and their parents were wealthy and put them in business, that was great. Some trained in the professional class—doctors, lawyers, and such. Otherwise, you became a salesman, selling cars or stocks or working as a manufacturer's representative. But you used the game of golf to enhance whatever your business pursuit might be.

In today's world, huge purses on the PGA Tour have decimated the ranks of amateur golf. Mind you, there is a wealth of amateur talent out there today. But most of those are college players and the best of that group are certain to pursue a professional career. There's hardly a decision to be made; there's too much at stake. The only young man I know who could have played professionally and who has remained an amateur is Trip Kuehne. He decided early on that the life on the PGA Tour was not suited to him, so he is working in the financial arena and plays top-level amateur golf. However, he is the exception.

Amateur golf in the 1950s was much bigger than professional golf. That changed toward the end of the decade when Jack Nicklaus came on the scene. His rivalry with Arnold Palmer ignited the professional game. Tournaments began to be shown on television and the audiences fell in love with one player or the other. Tournament purses began to escalate and the start of the modern era commenced.

Sponsorship of players came into vogue about this time. If a young man wanted to try his hand on the professional circuit, he often approached a group of businessmen—a syndicate—that would finance the player's pursuit in exchange for a percentage of his winnings. Staking a horse in that regard was more of a fun thing for the backers than it was an investment, and if the player became successful, he would buy out the shares in the syndicate and the backers were happy to let him do so. All they wanted was the success of the player. Billy Casper, around 1954, was the first player I ever heard of to have such an arrangement.

I worked at the automobile dealership for about a year

when I met two brothers from Alexandria, Louisiana. John and Charles Waters used to run a big tournament held on Labor Day each year called the Deep South Four-Ball. The Waters brothers hired me to go to work in their insurance agency, Fireside Mutual Life Insurance. These two men all but adopted me, and I could be working there today if I had wanted to stay.

The company was brand-new and my job was to sell stock in the firm. I'd go to people I knew and people I didn't know and try to convince them to invest in this new venture. I was not well suited to such a job. To be in sales, you have to be able to ask for the business and close the deal, and I was not good at either. Some people in golf are fabulous at sales, but I was uncomfortable, which is not a good thing for either the ego or sales output.

But the Waters brothers would do anything for me and liked me so much that I felt obliged to give it my best shot. Even at that, in less than six months, I had to make a life-changing decision. It was the spring of 1957 and I was play-ing in the Lake Charles Open, and on the eve of the tournament, I decided to turn professional. I had done a lot of introspection and, at age twenty-four, looked at where I had been and where I was going. Where I was headed seemed to be a dead end because I really didn't enjoy my job and I couldn't see it turning into a career.

So my first professional event was at Lake Charles, and I proceeded to make an 8 on the very first hole. I recovered and won $250 in the tournament, and those winnings staked me for another couple of weeks. By then I had entered the qualifying round for the U.S. Open, which was played at the Birmingham Country Club, in Alabama.

I was the low qualifier, having shot rounds of 73-66. So here I was, with a ticket to the U.S. Open at Inverness and no way to get there. My meager $250 was gone and I had nothing else. I went to a friend, an oil man named John B. Ferguson of Gulfport, Mississippi. He liked me and had bought me in a Calcutta pool once, and I remember I played well enough to make him some nice money.

Based on our previous mutual good fortune, I asked him to lend me $500 so I could go play in the U.S. Open. That was quite a sum for 1957, but he agreed, and off I went in pursuit of a major championship. At my first opportunity, I paid Mr. Ferguson back.

Match-Play Mentality

THE DIFFERENCE BETWEEN MATCH PLAY AND stroke play is the same as the difference between steak and lobster. Both are great, but it's a matter of taste.

The psychology is quite different for the two forms of competition. In match play, it makes no difference what your eighteen- or thirty-six-hole score is. It matters only that you win more holes than your opponent. In that regard, your focus is different. You are not comparing yourself to par or to the rest of the field. You have a single opponent and he has your undivided attention. Of course, you are pitting your game against the course conditions that day, but there are times when your thinking will change predicated on what your opponent does on a particular hole.

For instance, if your opponent plays before you and he hits his approach shot close to the hole, you might choose to gamble a little more than you might have if his ball ended up farther from the hole. Conversely, if your opponent hits his ball out of bounds or into a water hazard, you might play a little safer than normal. In both cases, you are trying to win or halve the hole rather than posting a score.

In stroke play, every shot counts because you have to add them all up and record a total at the end of the day. In that respect, you are not only playing against par, you are playing against the rest of the field. You want to relate as well as you can to par on a given day, but you also have an idea how you relate to the rest of the players, particularly if you are near the lead on the final day.

Most of my amateur golf was conducted at match play. I noticed that for some peculiar reason, in a match-play situation, I could find myself in the so-called zone more often than not. And when I was in that zone, I actually played over my head. For some reason, I could zero in on my opponent and focus on a single shot and a single hole. Nothing else mattered but winning that hole. I couldn't get that same kind of focus in stroke play.

I remember playing in the Southern Intercollegiate in 1953, and I was trying as hard as I could to figure out how to get a medal score out of myself. I singled out a player in my own threesome and I played him a match in my mind, trying to divorce myself from the medal play round, focusing on a match-play situation, attempting to get the most out of my round.

Later, as a professional, I learned that to make a nice check or to finish near the top on Sunday, you must change your focus. Each shot matters and affects the seventy-two-hole total and the end of the tournament. In match play, you can change your strategy depending on your opponent's result. In stroke play, you have a game plan for the entire eighteen holes, and if you are successful in sticking to your plan, you'll have a good score and a chance to advance on the leaderboard.

It helped that as a professional, I was playing for a check each week. The difference between birdie and bogey might mean the difference between steak and hamburger. That knowledge will help you focus on one shot at a time.

Rookie Hazing

OFF I WENT TO THE 1957 U.S. OPEN AT INVERNESS IN TOLEDO, Ohio, with a friend of mine from New Orleans, Jim Hyde. One night, after a practice round, we were standing at the hotel bar when I looked up and found that we were in rather auspicious company.

On the one side was Tommy Bolt and the other, the great Walter Hagen. They began to grill me as to why I would have the audacity to turn pro. Who did I think I was bringing my Mississippi golf game out with the greatest players in the world? They were tossing me up in the air, turning me around, and barbecuing me, having a great deal of fun at my expense. Here I was at my first U.S. Open and I was indoctrinated by two of the great reprobates the game has ever known.

I was paired in front of Hogan for the first two rounds and behind Jimmy Demaret. I was in a sandwich of two great players. Demaret was having a great year and was trying to win the Open for the first time. He wound up 1 shot out of the playoff between Cary Middlecoff and Dick Mayer, which was won by Mayer.

My golf, however, was not so great. I was paired with Don Cherry and Rex Baxter, and I shot 82-77. But my luck was not all bad at Inverness. My friend Jim Hyde had spent some time in the company of Ed Carter, who was the tour director for the PGA. He told Jim that Merion Golf Club near Philadelphia was looking for a young pro to serve as an assistant to Fred Austin. But his primary job was to be a playing pro—play with members, play in tournaments, play wherever it was thought he should play.

In those days, when you turned pro, you got yourself a job as a club pro at a place where the members liked you to play in tournaments. All the great players in the 1930s and 1940s, even into the '50s and '60s, had club affiliations. No one in those days could make a living just by playing tournaments.

So it was a natural progression that if I was to be a pro, I needed a job, and this one seemed ideal. I called the club and sure enough, they were interested in interviewing me. I went to Philadelphia from New Orleans with some of John Ferguson's money and met with the committee over a weekend. They hired me that weekend, and I didn't even go back to New Orleans. I started right away and finished the season there.

Almost fifty years later, I'm still at it.

Top-Drawer Tournament

THE COLONIAL INVITATIONAL WAS AN AMATEUR EVENT IN MEMPHIS in the 1950s and '60s, the likes of which this country had never seen. Under the auspices of Roy D. Moore, the tournament attracted the finest field of amateurs that I'd ever been a part of.

Moore, a publicist with the world-famous Peabody Hotel and other concerns in the Deep South, promoted the Colonial Invitational to benefit the Home for the Incurables in Memphis. The finals would draw as many as twelve thousand fans to watch some of the best golf in the country.

Through the years, the winners were all national-caliber amateurs. Hillman Robbins won the Colonial four times. I was fortunate enough to win in 1955, defeating Mason Rudolph in the finals. In 1959, the semifinalists were Jack Nicklaus, Deane Beman, Tommy Aaron, and Richard Crawford. Beman was a U.S. Amateur champion, Aaron had won the Western Amateur, Crawford was twice an NCAA Championship winner, and Nicklaus, of course, was Nicklaus.

Not only were the field and the competition incredible, so were the social functions. The players were housed at the

Peabody, one of the country's great hotels, and there was dancing under the stars each evening.

Moore was also a director of the Western Golf Association and attracted the Western Four-Ball to the Memphis Country Club. Hillman Robbins and I managed to win the last Four-Ball played there. It was a great tournament and it left a void in national-caliber amateur golf.

So did Moore. Without men like him, the golden age of amateur golf would have been poorer.

Setup

ONCE YOU'VE TAKEN YOUR GRIP, YOU LOWER the club to the ball by unhinging your hands at the wrists. When we say "ground the club," that can sometimes be a misnomer. If you truly ground the club, it becomes anchored there and you can't swing it. A better habit is to touch the grass behind the ball with the clubhead.

You adjust your feet for a sense of balance, and because your knees are flexed, your weight has settled between the heels and the balls of your feet. That weight should rest evenly, not toward your heel or the toes. You should be able to raise your toes and still swing a golf club. For most shots, the weight distribution should be about equal between your right and left leg. For longer shots, you might set more weight on your right leg, much like a baseball batter might if he was trying to hit one out of the park. For shorter shots, like chip shots or pitch shots, you might set more weight on your left leg.

Learning Curve

WHEN I WENT TO MERION GOLF CLUB, I RECEIVED A FABULOUS break. The club is rich with history, and the course is perhaps the architecturally best I have ever seen. I took the opportunity to learn about Merion and all the history that had been created there by Bobby Jones and Ben Hogan and all the other greats of the game who had played there in years past.

Merion gave me a great place to start a professional career. I learned how to hit shots and to become a better player. What's more, I gained an appreciation for our great game, which I really didn't have before. I had a passion for golf, but I didn't have a love and respect for the game until I had spent a considerable amount of time at Merion. And I got to know the wonderful membership at Merion, and I'm still friendly with many of those people I met there.

I learned that if I was to play professional golf among the game's best players, I needed to get better in a hurry. I was to compete with the likes of Ben Hogan and Sam Snead, and if that was to be my chosen profession, I should become the best player I could be. The problem was that I didn't quite know how. I turned pro to play golf, not to teach golf. I didn't set out to be a club pro, but in those days, you had to have a club job to survive financially. I never had a teacher and played the game by feel and intuition. I thought that's the way the game should be played. I really didn't believe in teaching and thought it was a waste of time. I had never given a lesson, never made the slightest attempt to teach anyone about the golf swing.

But I had a job at Merion, and not only was I being paid to be a playing professional, I was expected to teach as well. And I had a financial stake in my ability as a teacher—I needed the money. Through attempting to learn more about my swing, I learned more about the swings of others. The irony turned out to be that I began the process to improve as a player and wound up teaching the game for almost fifty years.

As a player, I learned that it is sometimes better to prosper from a failure than a success. I shot 82-77 in my first U.S. Open and discovered that I had a long way to go before I could compete. I played in a tournament once in Shreveport, Louisiana, and shot 88 in the first round. I had no idea why I played that way and thought it was the end of the world and I'd never play well again.

Then, almost overnight, things turn around and you find yourself playing better than ever. You might haul off and win something you had no idea you could win because you entered the event in a skeptical frame of mind. Many good tournament rounds are played by people who did not expect to do well. You play along, and without explanation, things get going and everything starts to feel right. After you add it all up, you have a good score. Odd things happen in golf, especially in tournament golf.

So yes, there's a lot that can be learned from adversity. Losing is not much fun, but something can be gleaned from the experience. The trademark of a good player is that if he plays a poor shot, he comes back with a good shot. If he makes a bogey or worse, he is liable to make birdie on the next hole. After a bad round, he is likely to shoot a good round. He'll follow a poor tournament with a great one. There's something inside good players that allows them to resurrect something good from something bad.

Ball Placement

I PREFER TO PLACE THE BALL JUST INSIDE THE left heel during the setup, and that should be a constant relationship for every club and every shot under normal circumstances. The reason is that it makes for consistency. You can vary the right foot by widening or narrowing your stance to ad-  just to the terrain and to give you a foundation from which you can swing. You swing the club the same way, but you can adjust the stance.

When you move the ball in your stance toward your back foot, you compound all the variables. The club will arrive at the ball sooner, so you don't have as much time to create clubhead speed, causing a weaker shot. Moving the ball toward your back foot can also affect the direction of the shot.

Beginning players won't have as much time to close the club-face, so their shots tend to fade or be pushed. More accomplished players tend to manipulate the hands early in order to close the face and they tend to hit more hooks. Also, when the ball is moved toward the back foot, the trajectory of the shot tends to be lower.

Changing the ball placement can also affect the legwork. The legs tend not to move laterally; if they did, you'd move completely past the ball. By playing every shot forward in the stance, you also encourage the right use of the legs.

Not many things good occur when you move the ball toward the back foot. So why not simplify things and keep the ball in the same position every time?

Fundamentals of Teaching

ABOUT THE TIME I GOT TO MERION, IN 1957, BEN HOGAN'S book *Five Lessons: The Modern Fundamentals of Golf* was beginning to be popular and wound up becoming very prominent on the teaching scene. I was caught up in the book, as were thousands of players and teachers. Still today, the book is a seminal text in the area of golf teaching.

I believe Hogan's book caused people to delve into instruction more so than any other book that had ever been written before and perhaps since. For the first time, people really wanted to know about the intricacies and mysteries of the golf swing—grip, setup, swing, and swing plane. The book wound up being a guide for me. A lot of the things that I began to try to teach—and still teach today—are based on the findings in Hogan's book.

After that, as I evolved into my own theory of Swing the Handle, I thought I had a better way of explaining those fundamentals than was presented by Hogan. Even as popular as the book was, I began to question some aspects, particularly pronation and supination. I believe that the role of the hands in the swing is passive, not active, and that the forearms swing the handle of the club over the right hip and then over the left hip.

As a beginning teacher, I exposed myself to a lot of teachers and listened to what they had to say, watched what they did, and tried to pick and glean the best of what I saw and heard, while trying to develop my own ideas.

Don't Stand Still

YOU HAVE TO KEEP IN MOTION WHILE YOU ARE setting your alignment. You waggle the club in your hands and wiggle your feet, which alleviates tension. Every joint in your body must be free of tension: the knuckles in your fingers, your wrists, your elbows—especially your elbows—the ver-  tebrae in your back, your hips, knees, ankles, and toes. Even your jaw. When you get tense and tight, the joints lock and you get paralyzed. If all the joints are not free, you can't transmit the swing.

With alignment, you set your body as parallel to the target line as you possibly can, beginning with the eyes. The eyes must be parallel to the target line. You can swivel your head to the right and to the left, but your eyes remain on that line. If your head swivels the wrong way, you will see the ball incorrectly. When your eyes are on that line, it makes it easy to set the shoulders, hips, knees, and tips of the shoes on that line.

Early Days on Tour

CONTRARY TO WHAT SOME MIGHT BELIEVE, WHEN I STARTED ON THE PGA Tour in the late 1950s, there was a full complement of about forty tournaments each year. The Tour started out west in January and wended through the Southeast in the fall and ended in south Florida into December.

In those days, I played a full schedule on the winter Tour, and you could play by participating in the Monday qualifiers. There would be 150 players in the starting field on Thursday, but there were as many as 50 spots for the Monday qualifier. It wasn't difficult to qualify. In fact, you had to post a lousy round not to get in. If you made the cut, that qualified you for the next tournament. The last tournament of the year was in December at Sanford, Florida, where the baseball Giants used to train in the spring. A couple of times, I was exempt for the Los Angeles Open at the start of the next season by virtue of the fact that I made the cut in Sanford.

In Beaumont, Texas, with nine holes to play in the final round, I was leading the tournament. I was pulling every switch I had to make myself play well on the last nine. It was almost like the experience in the Southern Intercollegiate in which I picked out a playing partner and played a match in my mind.

I couldn't quite put my finger on what to do, but that's what you see with these young Tour players when they're about to win. They haven't been there before and you don't know how they might react. But I shot 36 on the final nine and three players went by me. Joe Campbell won the tournament. It was his first win. Jay Hebert and I tied for fourth. Then it was on to Mobile, down to West Palm, and then to Miami. A Christmas visit with friends in Meridian and New Orleans preceded the West Coast tour.

I was not a great player by anyone's stretch of the imagination. But I was a solid player who enjoyed a modicum of success. I set the competitive course record at Medinah Country Club near Chicago in 1962. I qualified for the U.S. Open eight times. I played in the PGA Championship six times and the PGA Club Professional Championship six times. I won the Metropolitan PGA Championship and the Southern California Stroke Play Championship twice. I played in some two hundred PGA Tour events all together.

I had just enough success to satisfy me as a player. By 1962, I had taken the head professional's job at Bel-Air and my thoughts turned to teaching and serving my membership.

I still liked playing, but I didn't enjoy it as much as I had when I was an amateur. It wasn't the passion it used to be, and I found I enjoyed teaching just as much as I enjoyed playing. And as the years went on, I found I enjoyed teaching even more.

Two-Sided Swing

YOU CAN GO TO GREAT LENGTHS TO COMPLI-cate the swing. That won't enable you to play better or in a more enjoyable fashion. So here's the simplest way I know to swing a golf club.

The handle part of the shaft is in your hands. What can you do with the handle of the club? You can't eat with it, you can't paint with it, you can't write with it, and you won't lead the band with it. All you can do with that handle is swing it. The only parts of your body that can move the club in a consistent fashion are your forearms. Your two forearms combine to swing the handle of the club from one side of your body to the other, all the while keeping the joints in your body as free as possible.

It's akin to a tennis stroke. Let's say your club is a tennis racket. If you make a two-arm stroke, you use your forearms to swing the racket from one side of your body to the other. You do not flip the racket over with your hands. In fact, throughout the stroke, your hands remain to the side of the racket. That's exactly where they should remain in the golf swing.

Put a golf club and a tennis racket in your hands at the same time. You grip with equal but opposite pressure. You align your hands with the face of the club or racket. It wouldn't occur to you to flip your hands over unless you were trying to do something tricky. The tennis racket and the golf club are similar instruments in that they both have a handle, a shaft, and a head or face. The ordinary person does the right thing with a tennis racket. But the same person picks up a golf club and becomes fixated with the head of the club and tries to do something with the clubhead. There begin the problems.

Those problems will last a lifetime unless you realize that you should swing the club the same way you swing the tennis racket. If you can make this analogy, it will be helpful to you. It's a two-sided swing.

Education of a Golfer

I HAD A GREAT EXPERIENCE AT MERION WITH THE PEOPLE OF THE Philadelphia Main Line. There is a code there that probably still exists, though I would imagine it's not as stringent as it was when I was there. I can still see the way they dress. During the day, the men would come into the club in their gray flannel slacks and change into khaki pants, golf shirts, and cloth belts. The women wore the Lily Pulitzer line of flowered cotton skirts and the Lacoste shirts that are coming back into vogue today.

They were very proper in their manner, whether it was greeting friends or sharing a drink or a meal. To me it was quite impressive, a lad from Mississippi in the midst of the wealthy social class. And that code and manner translated into golf—we all knew at Merion that golf was a gentleman's game and was to be treated as such.

I learned the value of the navy blazer and the gray and camel slacks, the blue and white shirts, and the club and rep ties. The way they dress is actually very sensible. I notice that people who travel well and dress well do so very simply. You can get by with a navy blazer and a couple of pairs of gray slacks and khaki slacks and that's all the wardrobe you need for a week. Throw in a couple of blue and white dress shirts and you are all set. You don't have to have a new outfit for each day of the week. You can change the entire look of an outfit with a different necktie. The Main Liners, of course, take things to the extreme. They patch the elbows of their jackets and wear those tweeds until they fall off.

Not only are they conservative in their dress on the Main Line, they're also conservative in their money habits. It's altogether different from New York, although they are only ninety miles apart. The conservative air reigns supreme in Philadelphia and it's liberal in New York. Although I must say that there are a lot of similarities between the golf clubs in Philadelphia and New York. The way they dress and the rules they abide by and the schools they attend are remarkably the same. There are a lot of different campuses in the Ivy

League, but there's a lot of commonality among them. It's the same with Philadelphia and New York.

I wore golf clothes to work at Merion but always a jacket and tie if I went to dinner with some of the members. And later I took that mode of dress with me to California. When I took the Bel-Air job in 1962, I started a tradition of wearing a jacket and tie to work, whether in the golf shop or on the lesson tee. To me, it typifies what the game is all about. The people of Merion influenced the way I see the game and society as well as the way I dress for work or golf. It's the idea of being a gentleman at all times. Besides, the weather is pretty mild in Los Angeles and I don't have to change clothes several times a day.

I originally took the job at Merion so I could play in competition. I thought that's where my future lay. I've always enjoyed competition, and I thought I had enough golf game to play at the highest level. I imagine that if I won tournaments on the PGA Tour, I would have looked at that success and my place in it a little differently. But my highest finish was fourth at Beaumont, when I led the tournament with nine holes to play.

I must say, however, that I also enjoyed the social atmosphere of tournaments in those days. Players were all old friends. They traveled together, stayed in the same hotels, drank and dined together. It's much like the European Tour is today. But those days are gone on the American tour. There's too much at stake and players treat each event as a job. I don't believe that players have as much fun as the players of my era did. But they are making a whole lot more money. I guess there's a trade-off.

Because I was required to teach at Merion, I discovered a very important facet of my life: I actually enjoyed teaching. I liked the feeling I received from it. There was a sense of giving, and I didn't get that feeling from playing. I didn't get the same sense of satisfaction from tournament golf and I started to weigh one versus the other. When you teach, you are helping someone to help himself. When you are playing, you are satisfying yourself and that's about it. I think that's the difference.

I did play in some selected competition after I came to Bel-Air, but it wasn't much. The one thing that helped satisfy my competitive urge was coaching the UCLA golf team for fourteen years. It was a way to take my ability as a teacher and vent it through the medium of competition in which good players represented a team. The experience helped me as a teacher because we spent so much time in the science of playing the game—formulating strategies, learning how to keep a good round going, and salvaging a decent round from a potentially bad round—as opposed to just swinging and hitting shots.

One of a Kind

MOST OF US CAN COUNT ON ONE OR TWO HANDS THE REALLY GREAT friends we've had in our lives. Rex Cross is that kind of friend for me, and in that regard, he's certainly in the palm of my hand.

I met him at Westchester Country Club in New York when I was there for a brief stop before coming to Bel-Air in 1962. To tell you what kind of friend he was, he took me from Westchester to Doctors Hospital in New York when Lisa went into labor with our son Michael. And he held my hand at a German bar across the way while she was going through the pain of giving birth.

He spoke on my behalf to the Bel-Air people when I was being considered for the head professional's job. He is a member at Augusta National and has since become a member at Bel-Air and now lives in LaJolla, near San Diego.

Rex has always been a good player and was a close friend of Sam Snead, Jimmy Demaret, and Jackie Burke as well as many other touring professionals. Along the way, he befriended the legendary Bobby Locke of South Africa, known as perhaps the best putter who ever played the game. On one particular occasion, at our Swinging Bridge tournament at Bel-Air, I encountered Rex on the putting green and nearly mistook him for Locke.

As it happens, the two had been together in New York the weekend before. In the wee hours, after an all-night bout in one of New York's finer saloons, Locke had turned over the secret of his putting game and even gave Rex his heirloom hickory-shafted putter. And now Rex was demonstrating the Locke style with his new putter.

Locke believed in a closed stance, and he hooked his putts, which made them roll end over end more quickly, so that the ball would run true on any type of surface. He had an uncanny knack of rolling the ball so that it fell in at the edge of the hole. Locke told me once on a People to People trip to South Africa that when he came to America in the 1940s, he almost lost four of his first six tournaments. Which is to say that he won those events, much to the chagrin of the American tour pros.

But Locke is gone and Rex remains. Rex has Locke's putter and he has the keys to the secret of his style. So if you want to know more about Bobby Locke, you must contact Rex Cross.

I don't see Rex as often as I would like, but we have retained our friendship. Every time I have the opportunity to be in his presence, I become fully aware of how much his influence and his friendship have meant to me. I don't know if there is any way I could repay what he has done for me. But the great thing is that I know I don't have to because he would never want it that way.

Lost in the Backswing

MOST GOLFERS GET LOST IN THE BACKSWING;
they are too backswing oriented. There
isn't another game played that way. Any
other game you can think of, when the
ball is coming, you swing through the
ball. Tennis players and baseball batters
all swing forward. The football quarter-
back steps forward; bowlers think forward.

None of these players think backward, but golfers do. We
should downplay the role of the backswing and emphasize
the role of the forward swing. We use both forearms to make
the swing. Now, hold the club about halfway down the shaft
with the handle resting on your left hip. Without taking a
backswing, move the club to the left side of your body.
Swinging through the ball is the most important part of the
swing.

Notice that your hands remain to the side of the shaft at
all times. If you cause your hands to flip when you do this
drill, you cause a collision with the club and body. Your body
remains behind the shaft. We hear references to being behind
the ball. Behind the ball means little or nothing. You can be
behind the ball but out in front of the club. You can't play
from there. Behind the shaft of the club is where you want
to be.

Competitors and Friends

TWO CONTEMPORARIES WHOM I COMPETED AGAINST FROM THE junior ranks to the professional game are rarely mentioned, but both are great players and even better human beings.

Mason Rudolph of Clarksville, Tennessee, won the U.S. Junior in 1950, a year after losing in the finals to Gay Brewer. He also won the Western Amateur and competed on the Walker Cup team during what I refer to as the Golden Age of amateur golf. He was developed by O'Neal Buck White, who also had a hand in teaching Hillman Robbins. Mason spent a year at Tennessee and transferred to Memphis State, where he finished his college career.

Mason went on to become a professional and had a distinguished career. He was known for his straight shooting and his uncanny ability to chip and putt. He broke many a heart with that putter of his.

He and his wife, Carol, still live in their hometown of Clarksville, where they first met. He later became golf coach at Vanderbilt and still has a hand in the program's fundraising efforts. The townspeople love him so much that they named the town's golf course in his honor. It's only fitting.

Gay Brewer won the U.S. Junior in 1949, went off to the University of Kentucky, then on to the military, and turned pro in the middle '50s. He is a Masters champion and in the decades of the '60s and '70s was known as one of the best players in the game.

His swing, though quite effective, was never the prettiest

to look at, and he was always searching. He was looking for a swing thought, a new club, a new idea to make him play better that day and that tournament. He was a hard worker and was fiercely competitive. He never thought anyone could possibly be better than he was.

He and his wife, Carol, were good friends, and we had some nice moments—and memories—together.

Hand and Wrist Action

IT'S OF PARAMOUNT IMPORTANCE THAT YOU understand the relationship of the hands and wrists in the proper golf swing. Your hands and wrists are going to hinge upward and downward relative to the ball. You don't flap your hands, because that would cause the handle to go backward.  Neither do you try to roll the hands, the so-called release, because, again, you'd cause the handle to go backward.

Yet you can allow the vertical hinging to take place, and there's no conflict between club and body. If you were to hold a club in front of you and lift it over your head, here's what would happen: Your hands and wrists would hinge the club upward and your biceps would raise the club over your head. When you lower it back down, the triceps bring the club down and your hands unhinge at the wrists. That's as simple an act as you ever perform. That's how we lever the club up and down in the golf swing. It happens as naturally as can be.

The swing takes place in the forearms, and the body is behind the shaft at all times. When you move the club to the right, over your right hip, you allow your shoulders and hips to turn to the right and your body remains behind the shaft. Your first order of business is to move the handle to the left as soon as you can. If you delay it at all, your body tends to go first and you find yourself in front of the shaft. Any wrong movement in the swing will put you in front of the shaft.

Let's dream up all the wrong things that can happen in the swing. Let's say you start correctly and lay the club off in the backswing. You are in front of the club, where you don't want to be. If you do the opposite and hood the club going back, you are still in front of the club. If you are too flat, your body is out in front of the club. If you are too upright and out of plane, you are in front of the club. If you hit from the top, that puts you in front of the club. If you spin out and turn your body out of the way, that puts you in front of the club. If you release at the ball, you are in front of the club.

If you set up and stay behind the shaft during the swing, you are enjoying the best possible relationship between the club and body through the swing. The club is free of your body and all the body strength is set behind the club working to your advantage.

Why swing over the hips and not the shoulders? If you go over the shoulder, you are too high and above the plane, and the tendency is to come over the top because you're already over the top because you are too high. If you roll or flip the club, then you are below the hip and you are too low. It's over the hip on the right and over the hip on the left side. This keeps the club in plane (in position) throughout the swing.

Career Moves

I HAD BEEN AT MERION FOR THREE SEASONS. IN 1959, AT THE END of the third season, I went for the winter to Thunderbird Country Club in Palm Springs, California, to work for the legendary Claude Harmon. At the time, he had lost two of his assistants at Winged Foot in Mamaroneck, New York, and wanted to know if I was interested in one of those positions because I had been recommended to him. I was happy at Merion and didn't just want to swap jobs, but I was tempted by the opportunity to work for Harmon.

Claude Harmon was a guru among golf professionals in those days. He was credited, and rightly so, for getting plum jobs for dozens of his assistants over the years. It was a coup for any young professional to get such exposure to someone so influential. So I told him that if he invited me to Thunderbird for the winter, I'd take the assistant's job at Winged Foot. I was young and single, and the combination of seeing Palm Springs firsthand and the chance to work for Harmon was all but irresistible.

I arrived in Palm Springs in October 1959, just about the

time of the Ryder Cup matches at El Dorado. I remember watching those matches and wondering if the time would ever come that I might be playing for the American side. In the meantime, I was an assistant golf pro with no visible means of support. In those days, the assistant pros weren't paid in these winter jobs. I received no salary. We were living in some club housing in an orange grove and we got our meals in the clubhouse, but there was no paycheck. Whatever money we made playing and teaching was ours, but that was about it. I was there not to get rich but to be exposed to Harmon.

But even the lure of Harmon wasn't enough to keep me in the desert. I didn't like Palm Springs; it was too artificial. So I got the notion to head back east. I had contacted the people at Merion and they welcomed me back, if I wanted to come. I knew Harmon wouldn't like this turn of events one bit and that it might hurt me down the road. But that's what I had to do, and my mind was made up. I told the Merion people I'd play my way back to Philadelphia by playing the winter portion of the PGA Tour, and I'd be there in time for the spring opening.

As it happened, a prestigious job on Long Island had opened just after I arrived back at Merion. Dave Marr, one of Harmon's former assistants, was the head pro at Rockaway Hunting Club and he was leaving to play the Tour fulltime. This was May 1960; the season had started and they were without a pro. Marr and Mason Rudolph, another good friend of mine, had recommended me to Harmon for the Rockaway job. Harmon signed off on almost every job in the Metropolitan PGA section, and he graciously agreed. He in turn recommended me to Donald Grant, who in a couple of years would become the president of the fledgling New York Mets.

I knew nothing of Rockaway Hunting Club, didn't even know where it was, and I was a bit leery. Luckily for me, I had a friend, Francis Sullivan, who was Ben Hogan's attorney and a member at Merion. Sullivan checked out Rockaway Hunt and came back with a glowing report. So I met with Grant and the others on the search committee and decided to take the job. Off to New York's Long Island I went.

The members had started a program, under Grant's guidance, in which the club hired young professionals and encouraged them either to go play on Tour or graduate to bigger and better club jobs. They started with Shelley Mayfield in the 1950s, who was succeeded by Gil Cavanaugh, then Marr. Mayfield went on to Meadowbrook on Long Island and then to Brook Hollow in Dallas, both premier clubs. Cavanaugh followed Mayfield to Meadowbrook and wintered in Hobe Sound, Florida.

Then I came along and stayed for two years, and in the second year, I had a life-changing experience. I got married.

The Pro's Pro

HE WAS KNOWN AS "PRO-IE" BY HIS INTIMATES, AND THOSE CLOSE to Claude Harmon were many. He was as popular a golf professional as any the business has ever produced. He had a very loud public relations department in the form of his members from Winged Foot, Seminole, and Thunderbird. They sang his praises, as did virtually everyone with whom he made contact.

He was a rarity among golf pros—quite a raconteur and, most surprising of all, a check grabber of the first order. Most golf pros have quite short arms when it comes to picking up a check.

When he was the pro at Winged Foot in the 1950s and 1960s, Monday was the pro's day off. So it was for the New York Giants, Yankees, Jets, and Mets, along with the media who covered all those teams. Monday afternoons became a time when Harmon gathered all those forces at Manuche's, Rose's, Eddie Condon's, "21," P. J. Clarke's, and Toots Shor's.

Harmon was always in the middle, his masterful storytelling ability front and center as the athletes and writers took a day to soothe bruised bodies and egos. More often than not, the afternoons spilled over into the night.

Proie had a pipeline of assistant pros, many of whom went on to have stellar careers of their own, either as golf professionals or PGA Tour players or both. Dave Marr, Shelley Mayfield, Jay Riviere, Jimmy Burke, Jackie Burke, Al Mengert, Gene Dahlbender, Jack Lumpkin, Rick Rhoads, Jack Doss, Don Callahan, Rod Funseth, Dutch Hood, Bill Lawe, and John Hayes were among those numbered.

Harmon was quite a player, as well, having been the 1947 Masters champion. He also had some success in the PGA Championship when it was conducted at match play. As host pro for the 1959 U.S. Open, he finished fourth at Winged Foot under the watchful eyes of his members and even bested his idol, Ben Hogan.

But his greatest legacy is the job he and his wife, Alice, did in raising four sons. Claude Jr. (Butch), Craig, Dick, and Bill have gone on to make more than considerable marks on the game with their own teaching. They proudly carry on the Harmon name that their father worked so diligently to create.

Distance

IF YOU TOSS A BALL TO ANOTHER PERSON, YOU make it go a certain distance, and to do that, you apply a certain force. The same holds true of the golf swing. The length of the swing is immaterial. Most players think length of swing has a direct bearing on how far the ball goes.

If I throw a ball a certain distance, I don't think about how far back I take my arm. I am thinking about going forward and about how much force to apply to get the ball to go that particular distance. The degree of force determines the distance.

Pick a target and make a swing, thinking of nothing but the degree of force required to make the ball go that distance. Make a swing and take in the outcome. Whether the ball flew the right distance was determined by the amount of force applied to do the job. And I'll bet you never even thought about how far back you took the club. Top tennis players don't think about how far back to swing the racket. Baseball players think forward, not backward. Prize fighters don't think about a backswing; they are moving forward with applied force. Bowlers think forward, not backward.

We don't hit the ball going backward, we play by going forward. Address the ball and have a friend step on the ball. Place the club to the ball and push the ball with all your might. You feel a force emanating through your forearms trying to move the handle of the club through the ball with whatever degree of force you feel like.

Full force will account for full distance. Now try to play a half shot. If your full-force 7-iron goes 150 yards, then a half-force 7-iron should go 75 yards. But it's an accelerated force. There is no shot you play where you should decelerate into the ball. Indirectly you create clubhead speed, but directly you create force with the handle.

Instead of putting a speedometer on the clubhead, let's put a meter on the end of the handle, the hub of the club, marked 0–25 pounds of force. To get maximum distance, you might apply 25 pounds of force. But to play a little chip shot, you might apply 1 pound of force. You are technically making the same swing, but you are applying a different amount of force. This force emanates within the forearms.

Moving On

IN THE SECOND YEAR OF MY TENURE AT ROCKAWAY HUNT, I MET THE woman I would soon marry—the lovely Lisa. In May of 1961, I went into Eddie Condon's in New York City and was introduced to Lisa Mason by Peter Pesci, who ran the place. I had a date with someone else that evening and so did she, so it didn't seem that we were all that interested in each other. But one thing led to another, and shortly afterward we had a date.

Lisa was working as a hostess at a "private key club" called the Gaslight. Lisa was asked to go to Paris to open the new club there but chose to marry the "Lil Pro." She's pondered over that decision ever since!

On paper, our match might not have been ideal, as Lisa is outgoing and gregarious while I am quiet and reserved. Most would say both are understatements. We were married October 2, 1961, in the famous "Little Church Around the Corner" and had our reception at the old Park Lane Hotel. Then we went off to Bermuda.

It's been fun for forty-five years and we still love visiting "the Big Apple" and the Hamptons whenever we can!

Two things changed when I hit New York—my accent and my license plate. Driving through Manhattan for the first time convinced me that the Mississippi license plate and the Southern drawl had to go; neither would survive in the Big Apple.

Contrary to what you might think, I liked New York. The

saying goes, "The winners survive in New York." There's a lot of truth to that. I liked the vitality, all of the action. Going into the city was for me a lot of fun, day or night. I remember traveling on the Long Island Expressway and the Van Wyck Expressway coming into the city from Rockaway Hunt, thirty-five minutes any way you cut it. Seeing those big buildings coming out of the Queens Midtown Tunnel was thrilling to a boy from Mississippi. Working at Rockaway Hunt, I had a room on the second floor of the clubhouse. I'd lie awake at night and listen to all those big planes flying in and out of Idlewild Airport. It was all a part of the mystique of New York City.

One of our members at Rockaway Hunt was a man named William Blount of Durham, North Carolina, who was the chairman of Liggett and Myers, the tobacco giant. He had an office in New York and had seats to the Yankees games. He offered them to me several times, and they were great seats, behind home plate between the plate and the stadium club. Driving Lisa to her hometown of Poughkeepsie one day, I proposed in the car as we passed Yankee Stadium, an unusually romantic setting to say the least. Luckily for me, she said yes. Forty-five years later, we're still at it.

I was beginning to be conflicted about what direction my career was trying to take. I still loved playing and competition. But because of my own discoveries about the golf swing, I had a newfound enthusiasm for teaching.

And my responsibilities were different at Rockaway Hunt. At Merion, I had been an assistant professional, responsible only for playing with the members and giving a few lessons. Mostly I worked on my game in preparation for playing the tour. But at Rockaway Hunt, I was the head pro, and that came with a whole new set of challenges. All of a sudden, I was in charge of a staff, of running the pro shop, seeing to it that the members were happy. And I was giving a fair number of lessons, teaching the members some of my discoveries.

I stayed at Rockaway Hunt for a couple of seasons, resigning the job just after Lisa and I were married so that we could chase the Tour full-time. We had no responsibilities except to each other and we thought it was the best thing to do. I thought I could still play out there, and I was playing my best golf during that period of time.

But things changed irreversibly in 1962 when our first son, Michael, was born. Now I had a home, wife, and child. I had to begin to think in terms of them instead of selfishly pursuing my own playing career. The Bel-Air job became open and I accepted it when offered in October 1962.

Ironically, Claude Harmon had been contacted when Bel-Air was looking for someone to replace Joe Novak. Harmon encouraged Dave Marr to take the job. But Marr was playing on the Tour and playing quite well. I'll always be grateful to Dave for being such a good player.

When I settled into the routine at Bel-Air, I had pretty much concluded that the Tour life was not for me. Our second son, Mason, came along in 1964, and that sealed the deal. When I first arrived in California, I still thought I could hold the club job and play the Tour as well. That's the way everyone else who was successful had done it. Why not me?

My thinking began to change when I saw that there were more and more players who were making a living—a good living—by doing nothing except playing in tournaments. It's tough to go from the club atmosphere to the tournament atmosphere and expect to play consistently well. With more and more tournament players, the degree of mental toughness was getting higher by the year. You couldn't depend on your ability alone. The adjustment was too great and took too much time.

Playing at the highest level of competition had become a full-time job. It had become increasingly difficult to go back and forth. It's much easier to go from the higher level to the lower level. But the opposite now meant that you had to devote all of your time to that pursuit.

I have no regrets about the choice I made. Bel-Air gave us a base to establish and grow a home and raise our children. If I hadn't married and had children, then I probably would have continued to pursue the playing. In the beginning, I set out to be a player and to become the best player I could be. I had no idea that I'd learn to love teaching. But when I settled in here as a club pro, all of a sudden I was able to do the teaching that I wanted to do.

The Tour is intoxicating. And nothing has changed in that regard from that day to this one. I get a kick from being around the majors every year, even to this day. I like the reunions and, as a teacher, if you have a horse in the race, all the better. But it's good to come home. That's where I belong.

Wise Counsel

LIFE OFFERS YOU WHAT APPEAR TO BE COINCIDENCES PERIODI-cally. But if you pay close attention, they might not be coincidences at all, rather part of a grand plan. I have a connection between Merion, Bel-Air, and Ben Hogan, and I had great relationships with all. The common denominator for that connection is Francis W. Sullivan.

Sullivan was an attorney and a former district attorney in Philadelphia. He was a supporter of John F. Kennedy and helped elect him to the presidency. He was also one of the best friends Ben Hogan ever had.

He was also a member at Merion, and while I was there, he became a friend and almost a surrogate father to me. We remained fast friends until his death. We spent hours at Merion playing golf and discussing life. Later, he recommended me for the job at Bel-Air.

I thought so much of Sullivan that I asked him—and he agreed—to be godfather to my son Michael. When Michael was a page to the House of Representatives in 1979 during his senior year in high school at Loyola, he went to Philadelphia on his first free weekend to meet and spend time with his godfather.

Sullivan was also a great friend to Bob Hope. No two people could have been as different as they were—Sullivan, the epitome of a Philadelphia lawyer, and Hope, the epitome of Bob Hope. One lived by day, the other by night, but they enjoyed each other's company.

Sullivan was one of my most ardent supporters, and whenever I needed advice and counsel, I could count on him.

Direction

HOW DO YOU ACCOUNT FOR DIRECTION? IS IT alignment, as most people think? Is it the body alignment or the club alignment? If the ball goes off to the right, they think it must mean that the alignment was off to the right. Not so.

If you took a ball in hand and tossed it to me, how would you make it go in the right direction? You'd extend your arm toward me. Otherwise the ball would have no chance to travel that way. That's precisely what you want to do with the club. With both hands on the handle, when you swing the club through the ball, your right arm is extended toward the target, precisely as if you were tossing a ball. Your right arm has extended the shaft of the club, and whatever direction your right arm is pointed, that's the way the ball starts, without fail.

You can have a perfect sense of alignment. Let's say your eyes, shoulders, knees, and toes are in perfect alignment and the clubface is at a right angle to your target line. Yet if you extend your right arm forty yards to the right of the target, the ball goes forty yards to the right. You are dealing with physical fact: The direction of the extended force determines the direction of the ball. From the same sense of alignment, if the ball goes forty yards to the left, it can go there only if the right arm extends there.

First, play a little chip shot and chip the ball to a target, to become aware of what your right arm is doing. Your right arm extends the shaft toward the target. Now enlarge it into a full shot. Pick a target and make the ball go in the direction of the target by extending your right arm precisely there.

The Nickname

NOT BEING THE TALLEST PERSON ON THE COURSE MEANS THAT I'M bound to be called something other than my given name. Jacques Houdry, a member at Merion, one day called me "the Little Pro." And it stuck—with him, anyway.

When we went out and played the winter tour, I'd play a lot of practice rounds with Jerry Pittman, who was the pro at the Creek Club on Long Island, where Joe Dey used to play (it was Dey who got Pittman the job). Pittman later became the pro at Seminole. He kept calling me "the Little Pro" over and over. Now it stuck on Tour. I have been known that way ever since.

Houdry became a dear friend of mine and still remains so, having met me when I went to Merion in 1957. He was part of the group who helped to hire me there. He ended up being the best man at Lisa's and my wedding. We played a lot of golf together and have a wonderful relationship.

Jacques was a very fine player, having been the number one player on the Princeton team when Bill Campbell, the great lifetime amateur, went to Princeton. Jacques qualified and played in the 1950 U.S. Open at Merion. He was a son of Eugene Houdry, a French inventor who developed aviation gasoline with his famous Houdry process, which was designed to convert petroleum into aviation gasoline. He literally gave his fortune away to French relief during World War II, with the avowed statement, "I'll make it back," which he did.

Curve

THE STRAIGHT SHOT IS THE HARDEST IN GOLF. You are swinging the handle of the club in a circular motion and the clubhead is traveling in excess of one hundred miles an hour. To try to time it so that your clubface is perfectly square at impact time after time is more than most people can manage, even the most talented among us.

However, you can time it so that the face is a bit closed or a bit open. If you leave the face open, it touches the inside part of the ball. It's like hitting a cue ball with a pool stick on the left side. The stick imparts English and the ball spins to the right. That's precisely what your golf ball does. You try to time the swinging of the handle so that the clubface is a little open.

If you time the swing so that the toe overtakes the heel of the club, the clubface touches the outside part of the ball. It's like hitting a cue ball on the right side. It imparts English and spins to the left.

Mind you, you are not going to hook or slice the ball. That only happens if your hands get into the act, leaving the clubface extremely open or closed. By swinging the handle over each hip with your forearms, you leave the hands to their proper role. You draw or fade with the forearms; you hook or slice with the hands.

You shouldn't find yourself making a swing and looking up watching the ball with a question mark on your face, wondering what happened. The feedback from the ball in flight should give you enough information. You need to know the cause and effect.

Starstruck

THERE WAS A ROMANCE FROM AFAR ABOUT BEL-AIR. MERE MENTION of the name conjured images of movie personalities—Clark Gable, Bing Crosby, and all the rest. That's how the club was known.

I played there once as an amateur in 1956, having come out to Los Angeles for the Rose Bowl. After my little stint in the military, I joined LaGorce Country Club in Miami as a junior member and met Bill McDonald there. He was also a member at Bel-Air and manufactured house trailers. After the Junior Chamber of Commerce defaulted on sponsoring the Los Angeles Open that year, McDonald picked up the sponsorship to keep the tournament alive. He wound up inviting me to the tournament to play on a sponsor's exemption. I played golf the morning of the Rose Bowl—UCLA versus Michigan State—with McDonald against Tim Holland and Al Besselink, a Tour player who was known for going deep into the night. We won $17, and I haven't collected yet.

I had been around famous people early in my career. I had played in the Crosby Pro-Am and I had played in New York with a number of celebrities, so I was not awestruck, but you couldn't help but notice who these people were. So I was impressed with those stars, but there were also a large number of people who were successful athletes, businessmen, and professional people. It was a heady experience for a boy from Mississippi, but I had been well trained in Philadelphia and New York, so I was not caught completely by surprise.

The employment situation at Bel-Air was another thing entirely. In the early days, I wasn't being paid a salary. That's the way it was in those days. The income from the golf shop was mine, as were the bag storage fees. There was no driving range and I received no revenue from golf cart rentals, as was the case at other clubs. I had income from golf lessons and whatever I might make playing in tournaments and any endorsement income from equipment or apparel manufacturers.

It has been a great opportunity and the people at Bel-Air have supported me from the beginning. They patronized the golf shop and encouraged my pursuits as a player. They might even take up a collection for my expenses when I'd go off to the U.S. Open or PGA Championship. Later, in 1975, when I was asked to coach the golf team at UCLA, the membership at Bel-Air was completely in my court. It was up to me to see that one job didn't conflict with the other, and we made a pact that wouldn't allow that to happen.

We have two great institutions in our neighborhood on either side of Sunset Boulevard—UCLA and Bel-Air. If we can complement one another, that's a big gain for everyone. I was even able to get some of our members to support the UCLA golf program. It really helped both institutions. I am proud of that.

Raconteur Extraordinaire

PETER PESCI USED TO OPERATE EDDIE CONDON'S NIGHTCLUB, A favorite hangout for New Yorkers and others who liked to gather and listen to music and to encounter friends who were in town to visit. It was a favorite haunt for football players, basketball players, golfers, baseball players, you name it.

It was a *Guys and Dolls* haven of the first magnitude. Pesci was a great friend of Dave Marr, Frank Gifford, and Charlie Connerly of the New York football Giants and the great Yankee players Mickey Mantle, Whitey Ford, Billy Martin, Yogi Berra, and Roger Maris. Many of these athletes liked to assemble on Mondays, which was the day off for golf pros and football players. They gathered at Eddie Condon's to have a few drinks in the afternoon, dinner in the evening. Then decisions were made as to where to go next.

All of the above was presided over by Pesci, who was one of the majordomos who knew everyone in New York and beyond. If you wanted to know who was in town, the first stop was Eddie Condon's to get the lowdown from Pesci.

When Peter died, Lisa was on hand at the wake, held in lower Manhattan. Many friends and many more athletes attended to pay their last respects. Lisa and Gifford were standing guard in the funeral home when they decided to see if Peter was wearing his famous red socks, which he always wore. They lifted the pant legs in the casket and sure enough, there they were, the bright red cashmere socks.

The next day, at the funeral on Long Island, Bel-Air member Pierre Cosette had been picked up in a limousine by Bill Fugazy, who ran a limo company among other things. They were scheduled to be playing golf that day, but Fugazy decided to drop by Pesci's funeral and go out to the cemetery. Lisa was paying her last respects at the grave site when she looked across the way and saw Cosette, in golf clothes, standing idly by another headstone, wondering what he was doing at the interment of a man he didn't know.

So she ambled over and asked Cosette, "What in the world are you doing here?"

"Dear," he said, "I don't know. I was just on my way to play golf with Fugazy and here I am."

Pesci's wife, Martha, was a good golf player. She and I were once paired in a Pro-Lady tournament in New Jersey, and we played our way into the finals against Tommy Bolt and Lajunta White, only to lose 1-down on the eighteenth green.

On the first tee, Bolt suggested that we pyramid the money. Instead of having a winner's check and a runner-up's check, we agreed that we'd combine the two and play the match for the whole thing. At the end, I endorsed my check over to Bolt, but Martha was not on hand to witness things. As I drove back to New York that night with Peter, Martha, and Lisa in the car, Martha said, "Well, at least I helped to win a second-place check."

I told her that we had wagered both checks on the final match. She almost had a heart attack. And to this day, Lisa hasn't forgiven me.

The Saga of Bobby May

THE SCENE WAS THE VALHALLA GOLF CLUB ON AUGUST 20, 2000. The PGA Championship was being treated to a duel in the sun the likes of which had never been recorded. Tiger Woods was seeking the third leg of his heralded Grand "Tiger" Slam. Having captured the U.S. Open at Pebble Beach by a rousing 15 strokes and the millennium British Open at St. Andrews by 10, Tiger was enjoying his greatest year. After three rounds in the PGA, Woods was the leader at 13 under par.

Paired with Tiger for the final round and one stroke back was a relative unknown to the golfing world. Bob May was playing his very first PGA. Bob had earned his way into the Championship by being in the top 10 on the European Tour in 2000. He had recently won the British Masters.

That Sunday afternoon, a duel lasting five hours unfolded before the largest television audience ever to witness a golf tournament. The golfing world got to see a battle reminiscent of David and Goliath!

Tiger bogied the first hole, Bobby birdied the second—and just like that, David was ahead of Goliath. It would be the last bogie for either player, with many birdies to come. Making the turn in 35 and 36, the two Californians spent the next three hours in a zone that was a joy to watch and unbelievable to behold. Courtesy of CBS television, millions saw Woods and May exchange birdie for birdie and shot for shot like two great stage performers playing off one another and bringing out the best each had to offer. At the eighteenth green, Bobby took the lead by holing a snaky 12-foot putt from the rear of the green. Tiger, faced with sinking a fast-breaking 6-footer or being relegated to second place by this comparative unknown, rolled his putt as true as could be into the middle of the hole. They were tied!

Both players shot 31, five under par on Valhalla's difficult back nine for a four-round total of 270, eighteen under par and a new scoring record for the PGA Championship. But the day was not over. A new three-hole playoff had been called for in the event of a tie at the end of regulation play. Valhalla's final three holes were selected. The stage was reset, and the players were ready. A champion would be crowned—who would it be?

Fatigue may have been a factor into the fifth hour of competition: Both players became erratic off the tee, with only one of the six ensuing tee shots finding the fairway. Woods did so on the sixteenth hole (the first playoff hole) and proceeded to hole a 25-foot birdie putt after Bobby had almost holed a fantastic pitch shot out of the rough and up a slippery slope, with his ball coming to a stop two inches short of the middle of the hole. Tiger drove into the trees on the right at 17; Bobby countered by pulling his tee shot toward the bunker in the left rough. Each recovered for a spectacular par. At the eighteenth, Tiger hit a high pull deep into what appeared to be an abyss on the left. On television, his ball seemed to disappear unaccountably into the depths, only to come bouncing back into an opening shot off the fairway. Bob, given new life, again pulled his tee shot into the left rough. Tiger, having escaped disaster in Houdini-like fashion, advanced his ball up the fairway on this exacting par 5. Bob countered with a shot from the rough to the right side, leaving a tricky third shot to the flagstick, which he managed to put onto the green some 40 feet from the cup. Tiger, firing at the hole with his middle iron approach, caught the guard bunker before the green. He then blasted a lovely sand shot within three feet of the hole. Bob's birdie effort turned just below the hole, and the epic day concluded as Woods parred for his "Third Leg" Championship. Suffice it to say, neither player lost. A winner was to be determined, and history proves it was Tiger Woods. David didn't slay Goliath this day, but he did capture the golf world.

This second-place finish is atop a long list of second-place finishes for Bob May, including some twenty-five professional tournaments worldwide. With another twenty-five or more amateur, college, and junior tournaments where he finished second, Bob has had more near-misses than he would care to count.

Bob, at age thirty-five, is facing back surgery in the middle of his career. Let's hope for the best, because a career of dedication is as yet unfulfilled. Having worked with him since he was eleven years old, I have witnessed Bobby golf as a junior, an amateur, and a professional. He still has great promise.

To Practice or Not to Practice?

PRACTICE MAY NOT MAKE YOU PERFECT, BUT it goes a long way toward getting you closer to your goals. *How* you practice can make your journey shorter and your results more fulfilling.

One of the attributes I spotted in Bob May as a twelve-year-old boy was his penchant for practice. After a round that was not so pleasing, he never ran off to the beach or the nearest girlfriend. Instead, Bobby would head for "The Big Tee" driving range in Anaheim and pound golf balls until his mother called to claim him.

This kind of work ethic is admirable, to say the least. Dividends will come if it can be supplemented with good instruction.

How much time should be spent practicing? No slide-rule application seems to fit, because each individual player, whether he is a novice or a tour professional, has a different appetite for practice. I know of no player who ever killed himself with overindulgence in practice, yet no one became U.S. Open Champion without practice. Each player finds his own limit.

I would like to offer two areas for your practice consideration. First, the makeup of a golfer consists of four aspects: *mental, physical, technical,* and *spiritual. Mental* deals with all the emotional components (attitude, motivation, temperament, etc.). *Physical* consists of the physical well-being of the player (strength, flexibility, diet, rest habits, indulgences). *Technical* pertains to the golf swing and the knowledge thereof. *Spiritual* applies to the character development of a person. The combination of these four aspects makes a complete golfer.

The second area relates to the different departments of shot making: *driving, approach shots, short game,* and *putting.* No one of these departments is more important than any other because they are all interdependent. Practice time should be divided equally among these four areas.

Now you are complete as a golfer—and on your way to being the best you can be!

Walter O'Malley

BORN AND RAISED IN NEW YORK POLITICS AND SCHOOLED AT THE University of Pennsylvania, Walter Francis O'Malley gained his notoriety with the colorful Brooklyn Dodgers.

After O'Malley convinced his friend Horace Stoneham that, as Greeley said, it was time to move west, he and Stoneham said good-bye to New York and hello to the golden state of California with all its promise. They had the blessings of the national league and the baseball commissioner's offices.

Who would go north and who would go south was left to the two owners to decide. Using his political cunning to full advantage, O'Malley offered the first choice to Stoneham, knowing full well the sophisticated lure of San Francisco would draw the Giants. This left O'Malley and the zany Dodgers their new home in la-la land, with its magnificent weather and its millions of potential fans.

Stoneham must have wondered later, as the cold winds whistled through Candlestick Park off San Francisco Bay, whether he had been snookered by his cigar-smoking counterpart, who was now comfortably ensconced at Chavez ravine. But that's another story.

O'Malley did not learn his golf in Brooklyn (or maybe he did, evidenced by his handicap). He came into the golf world as a member of Los Angeles Country Club. The club does not allow showmen, yet they got one of the greatest. O'Malley also became a member of Hillcrest, where he boasted of being the token Irishman in a Jewish stronghold.

Within the framework of these clubs, he built a base of support for all the political, financial, and community projects necessary to build the Los Angeles Dodgers into the model organization in American sports. Talent like Koufax, Drysdale, and Scully certainly did not hurt.

My golfing experience with Walter O. was highlighted during trips to Dodgertown in Vero Beach, Florida, with members of the golf and poker club that he hosted every two or three years. Some fifty men boarded the Dodger airplane "Kay O II," named after his beloved wife, and off we went for three days of mayhem. The madness included eating, drinking, cards, golf, and storytelling.

Gin rummy began as soon as the wheels were up and continued through the trip until all but one was eliminated. On this particular trip the Little Pro survived to play the final match on the return flight against O'Malley in his compartment on his plane and with his rules, which included cigar smoking. What chance did I have? I didn't care to jump, so I settled for second place.

Golf at Dodgertown was unlike golf anyplace else in the world. The course included Florida's only par-6 hole, designed by Walter "Trent" O'Malley. The tight tree-lined fairways were made even tighter as the designer laid the water line down the middle of the fairways, creating a mounding effect that caused long, straight drives to bound oddly into the bordering palmetto bushes. All to the delight of Walter "Trent," who was ever protective of his twenty-two handicap for gaming purposes. His 180-yard drives were never affected by such trivia.

According to O'Malley, rules at Dodgertown were meant for others. He would make them on the spot, depending upon the circumstances. If he didn't like his lie, he would impose a casual water free drop rule after relieving himself on the lie.

Lies were the vogue at Dodgertown, and they were told well into the night in the poker room. Sleeping was not a fad with Walter F., and he was not interested in anyone else having such an unfair advantage. After a late night he was up at dawn and into his golf car for a horn-blaring, whistle-blowing ride through the encampment to make sure no one else was caught sleeping through the start of another fun-filled day.

Every year, my wife and sons were invited with me to join O'Malley at Dodger Stadium for dinner in his box suite during a game. It was a treat I will always cherish, with memories of one of the greatest men I have had the privilege of knowing. He treated the most insignificant like royalty and had his own way of bringing the high and mighty down to earth and causing them to like it. Life was a game, and his game was baseball. May his memory live on.

Don't Always Take a Man at His Word

IN 1992, FEELING MY OWN GOLF GAME WAS NOT WHAT IT COULD and should be, I did an introspective search. Was my playing condition mental, physical, or technical? Concluding that my hand-eye coordination was not exactly what it should be, I sought out the best available eye doctor to help me.

Dr. Robert Hepler, head of ophthalmology at UCLA's Jules Stein Clinic, was recommended. After an initial consultation, we made a date for a thorough examination two weeks later.

Three days after the consultation I received a beautiful letter from Dr. Hepler as a follow-up. I was now convinced beyond any doubt that I had found the right man. He suggested that I bring a driver to my upcoming appointment. He didn't suggest I bring a putter, an iron, or a wedge. He told me in no uncertain terms to bring my driver, which was the longest club in my bag. He must have reasoned, I concluded, that any deficiency would be more pronounced with the longer club. I was sold—and he was a nongolfer, no less.

On the morning of my appointment I went by my golf shop at Bel-Air and selected a brand-new driver for the occasion; the price tag was still attached. My wife, who accompanied me, was thinking, "What a nice gesture on Eddie's part, to take his new doctor a gift."

As the three of us—Lisa, the driver, and myself—entered the waiting room, other patients wondered why this crazy guy would be bringing a golf club to a doctor's office. Little did they know.

When Dr. Hepler saw me, he realized what had happened and burst into laughter. "I meant to bring a driver to drive you home after the examination," he stated. My story spread like wildfire through the UCLA community. I was a laughingstock. The new driver was mounted and hung on Dr. Hepler's office wall like a big trophy fish, its price tag still dangling. The Little Pro paid the price for his naïveté!

Trajectory

THE CLUB YOU CHOOSE AND THE DESCENDING stroke you make impart the backward spin that makes the ball rise in the air. Your arms lever the club up and down in the swing, and your hands hinge at the wrists to make contact with the ball.

Line up four or five balls on the grass and, holding a club, tap each ball on the top with the club-head, moving from one to another. That's exactly how you make contact with the ball—you hold the club at the handle and unhinge your hands at the wrists, thereby lowering the club to the ball. Your hands and wrists shouldn't flap sideways, nor should they roll from one side to the other in the so-called release.

Address a ball on the ground and make a swing over the top of the ball, without touching the ball. What you've done is make a perfect golf swing without having stopped to make contact with the ball. It's not like Monopoly in which you go from Atlantic Avenue to Baltimore Avenue and stop at Boardwalk in between. You are going from Atlantic to Baltimore in one swing.

You've created the swing. Now you have to lower the club to make contact with the ball. Swing the handle from one side to the other and make contact without stopping to meet the ball. The contact is made on the downswing. One of the worst habits golfers have is trying to help the ball into the air by hitting the ball on the upswing. You wouldn't do that with any other object. If I lay a tee on the ground and ask you to swing through the tee, you'll do it every time without trying to lift it into the air. Put any other object there and you'll do the same. You shouldn't treat the golf ball any differently, but many golfers do.

You simply want to swing directly through the ball by swinging the handle of the club from one side to the other. To help you with this concept, think of touching the ground beyond the ball when you make contact. You've got the full face of the club on the ball and have created the backward spin that made the ball rise in the air.

In the case of a tee shot, stick a tee in the ground and make a swing, simply knocking the tee over. Now place a ball on that tee and do the same thing: Knock the tee over. You will have made the same swing with the ball present that you did without the ball on the tee.

Jerry West

WHEN JERRY WEST RETIRED FROM PROFESSIONAL BASKETBALL AT age thirty-four after a long and fruitful career with the Los

Angeles Lakers, I think in his mind he thought he might be able to make the switch from basketball to golf and become a recognized tournament player. He was as low as a plus-2 handicap in those days and played Riviera and Bel-Air like he owned them. In fact, he played Bel-Air's famed back nine in 28 strokes once upon a time. He is the only player in the history of the club to have broken 30 on the back nine.

Interestingly, when he had the time to devote to his golf, I think he let his sense of pride get in the way. Even though he loved to play and no one was a better competitor, I believe he shied away from high-level competition for fear he'd shoot some embarrassing scores. I truly think this reticence on his part stood in the way of him becoming a fine player. Beginning at age thirty-four, he had about ten years in which he could have played on a high amateur level.

Jerry is an interesting study. He is one of the great competitors of all time, and if you had a team, he's the kind of player you'd choose first because he's in it to win. But winning in basketball can be expressed differently from in golf. In basketball, a player can take out his emotions on the court. If he's mad, he can grab a loose ball, make a steal, or take a rebound away from the opposition. He can use that emotional surge as a fuel to make him play even harder.

You can't play defense in golf. The fuel must be kept inside and the emotion contained. I don't think this was Jerry's nature. Maybe if he had played golf at an early age he might have developed that trait. He's a great athlete and has plenty of natural ability. He has the desire to practice and enjoys it. He really likes to play and is more than willing to play for a dollar or two. He has a group at Bel-Air that welcomes his challenge as much as he welcomes theirs.

When Jerry learned to play at Riviera, he developed what I term a "shut-to-open" swing, in which he closed his clubface somewhat on the backswing, opened it on the forward swing, then attempted to keep the face from turning away from the line of flight. As time went on, he worked with me and others, including Jimmy Ballard—to whom Jerry gave a lot of credit in developing his golf game—and he learned to swing his club more open to shut.

In my way of thinking, that's a more natural way to swing because you're swinging your club and turning your body in the same direction at the same time. When you swing from shut to open, you turn the club to the left and turn your body to the right. When you reverse the club, you do the opposite. That's not very natural.

Now sixty, Jerry is still working on his golf swing from day to day looking for the Holy Grail. He's still a natural athlete, and if you look closely at the NBA logo, you'll find that silhouette looks a lot like Jerry West.

Double Duty

IN THE BEGINNING AT BEL-AIR, I STILL PLAYED QUITE A BIT. I ended up playing in the Los Angeles Open fifteen times and participated in sixteen Crosby Pro-Ams because Bing was nice enough to invite me every year. I played in the San Diego

Open a number of times because Andy Williams was a member at Bel-Air and he had his name attached to the tournament. He invited me several times and I qualified a few more times. And I qualified to play in the Bob Hope Desert Classic several times.

From the time I turned pro in 1957, I tried to play as many Tour events as I could without jeopardizing any club pro situation I was in. In all, I played in more than two hundred Tour events. I'm a competitor and I love the challenge of testing myself to the fullest. I took what I believed in as a player and a teacher and displayed it on a stage that features the best players in the world. You really measure yourself at that point. To play with the best as an equal is very satisfying.

When you qualify to play in the U.S. Open or the PGA Championship, you have a very proud feeling that you deserve to be there, that at that moment you are one of the 150 best players in the world. That is a great compliment. But when you add it all up, most of the income I made from tournament golf I poured back into expense money to play more tournament golf. I spent more money chasing tournaments than I gleaned out of them. But it was a great education and I don't regret one moment or one dime spent.

I've always felt that any golf professional should exhaust his potential as a player to the nth degree to see how far he can go. When you see many of today's teachers, people who have gained a reputation as great teachers, sometimes you wonder about the depth of their ability as players. How can they be qualified as the best teachers in the world if they haven't competed in play against the best in the world?

At times, a teacher with a great reputation is called upon to teach someone with an even larger reputation as a golf player. In such a case, I think the teacher can be intimidated by the student. The teacher, in those cases, needs to have been in the heat of battle as a player so that what he imparts to his famous student carries some weight.

Jerry Barber

AS A NEW GENERATION OF GOLFERS COMES ALONG, I'M SOMETIMES afraid that noteworthy members of my generation will become forgotten. Jerry Barber is one of those personalities.

Barber stood only five foot five, but his slight frame did little to hide the fact that he had the competitive spirit of Goliath. He was the Corey Pavin of his time. Never long enough off the tee, Barber made up for that shortcoming with laserlike long-iron play and a short game second to none. He was never afraid to take on all comers.

A native of Illinois and raised to believe that you get what you work for, Barber had a tremendous work ethic. In fact, he was once spotted beside a Los Angeles freeway swinging his weighted club as he waited for the auto club to rescue his Cadillac that had broken down on the side of the road.

That Cadillac had the license plate "1961 PGA," a reference to his lone major championship victory, the 1961 PGA Championship at Olympia Fields, near Chicago. Don January was the victim of Barber's last-minute onslaught. January, with three holes to play, looked as if he would win his first major championship. But Barber, in the "Miracle at Olympia Fields," made putts of 20, 40, and 60 feet on the final holes to tie January and force a Monday playoff. Barber won the playoff with a 67 to edge January by 1. January would go on to win the 1967 PGA.

When told that he was a lucky so-and-so, Barber countered with his patented answer, "Yes, and the harder I practice the luckier I get." Never one to take no for an answer, Jerry had a strong opinion on any topic from love to politics.

Jerry met his match in 1966 during the Sahara Invitational in Las Vegas. He had an extra ticket to a title fight and he invited my wife, Lisa, because he enjoyed her company more than my own. He had no idea what he was in for. At a sporting event with Lisa, elbows to the back and ribs are all part of the bargain. An exhausted Jerry Barber had learned his lesson with black-and-blue marks to show for it.

Barber and I played together often, either in casual rounds in Los Angeles or competitive rounds in various championships. He couldn't get enough in practice rounds with Eric Monti, Bud Holscher, Mac Hunter, Jon Gustin, Jerry Pittman, J. C. Snead, and myself. We served as the sparring partners for the likes of Doug Ford, Arnold Palmer, Dow Finsterwald, and J. C. Snead's Uncle Sam. Never giving or asking an inch, Barber would try to overcome the competition he had chosen or else!

Paired with Jerry in the Southern California PGA Stroke Play Championship in 1975, I managed to win the tournament, surviving the needles and good-natured barbs of

Barber. I felt as though I had just won the English Channel Swimming Race with a weight attached to my legs.

As captain of the 1961 Ryder Cup team, Jerry, on the boat trip to England, decided to impose his will on the team with mandatory team meetings, practice sessions, and physical training. His teammates (Palmer, Littler, Ford, Finsterwald, January, et al.) had other, less strenuous training ideas in mind. A mutiny almost ensued and, fortunately, they did not throw him overboard.

With his regimen of exercise, vitamins (he consumed them by the dozens), and no alcohol or caffeine, Jerry should have lived to be one hundred. Because he was skeptical of doctors he did not anticipate the heart failure that brought on his premature death at age seventy-eight. (Exactly one month before, he carded a 70 in the first round of his last PGA Senior event, 4 shots out of the lead.)

Competitive until the very end, he was displayed by his sons Tom and Roger at his funeral service as we remember him: his horn-rimmed glasses, gold golf shirt, "J.B." baseball cap, royal blue polyester pants, best toupee, and a permanent smile. At the ready and buried with him were the tools of his trade—his old anvil putter with all the notches, his spare-time weighted training club, his favorite driver, and the ever-present writing pen ready to take your order.

The Ball

BEFORE YOU DO ANYTHING WITH THE GOLF shot, consider how the ball lies. It can be sitting on top of the grass, in a divot, deep in rough grass, or on bare dirt.

Noticing the lie of the ball can have a relaxing effect. It's like tossing a ball in the air and catching it. Your eyes are focusing on the ball and your subconscious takes over in the act of catching it. You do the same thing when you prepare to hit a golf shot. You focus on the ball and how it lies and then consider what kind of shot you are going to play.

You then understand how to make contact between club and ball. For instance, if you have a downhill lie, you make some adjustments. You adjust your shoulders to fit the slope of the terrain, and you might move the ball back in your stance because the bottom of the swing will occur a little higher on the slope, and you might move some of your weight toward the forward leg. You realize that the ball is going to fly a little lower off that lie because the club is slightly delofted at impact.

For a lie in the rough, you might need a little bigger swing when the ball is down in the grass. A bigger swing gives you more leverage up and down in relation to the ball. But you don't want the ball to go too far, so you might need a little slower swing tempo.

Lie is the first thing PGA Tour players notice before they

play a shot. It dictates everything you plan to do with the ball.

Hale Irwin

THERE'S NO QUESTION THAT HALE IRWIN IS A GREAT ATHLETE, even at age sixty-five. He has always kept himself in tip-top shape, and his swing has not changed much over the years. That's why he still dominates the Champions Tour, ten years past the day he first became eligible.

I saw him much earlier in his career, at his first tournament as a professional, in fact. We were paired together for the first two rounds of the 1970 Los Angeles Open. A year later, we were paired for the first two rounds of the PGA Championship at PGA National in Palm Beach Gardens, Florida, an event won by Jack Nicklaus.

The week before, he threatened to win at Tucson, where there had been a rain delay and a Monday finish. He didn't arrive at the PGA until Tuesday, where I clearly remember seeing him looking over the pairings. He saw that he was paired with me and wondered aloud why he didn't get a better pairing. "What did I do to deserve this?" he said.

We shared a laugh about that years later when Irwin and Raymond Floyd were the cohonorees for the Friends of Golf in 1990.

I was watching Irwin practice at the Los Angeles Open and it occurred to me that he had a wonderful golf swing, but I wanted to talk to him about his sense of rhythm. I wanted to see him slow his club down at the end of the backswing. He was fast in the transition. I gave him a little cadence that he could say to himself. At the end of the backswing, I wanted him to say "Set." And then I wanted him to say "Swing" at the ball.

"Set" and "swing." It makes for good rhythm. The two words have real meaning because you need to be "Set" in order to "Swing" on beat.

Testing a Theory

WHAT I DISCOVERED ON THE PRACTICE TEE AT MERION IN 1959 I tried to translate into the practice tees all over the PGA Tour at the various tournaments where I played. I never try to teach something until I have tested it in competition so that I can make sure for myself that it's right. I was convinced that what I was working on in my own game, and therefore had conveyed to others in my teaching, was really on the right track.

What's more, I didn't believe anything like it had been taught before. Most teaching up until then focused on the hands and the clubhead. I believed that the forearms should control the handle end of the club, which I now call the hub of the club.

In 1959, I approached Prentice-Hall with the idea of publishing a book about swinging the handle of the club. I had a completed manuscript and the publisher received it politely.

But I didn't have a name or a reputation that would sell books. In those days, you had to be Tommy Armour or Sam Snead to be a success at selling golf instruction in published form. It was known that most of those books were ghost-written, but the name still was the selling tool.

So nothing happened until 1972, when Bill Davis, the president of *Golf Digest,* came to Bel-Air as a guest of Dick Hauserman, a member here who had been a student of mine. Hauserman suggested to Davis that my theories concerning the golf swing were worthy of his consideration and that they should be published. Hauserman was friendly with Bob Toski, who was on the *Golf Digest* teaching staff, which helped the situation along.

Davis became interested and convinced the magazine's editors that they should do a book. At the time, *Golf Digest* did only two books a year and mine would be one of them in 1973. They came up with the title *Swing the Handle* because it was short and succinct and, besides, it sounded good. "Swing the Handle End of the Club" was too cumbersome. Dick Aultman, one of the instruction editors at *Golf Digest,* helped me write the book.

That led to my inclusion in the *Golf Digest* teaching panel that included Toski, Snead, Cary Middlecoff, Byron Nelson, Henry Ransom, John Jacobs, and Jim Flick. That was some pretty lofty company for someone like me, but I felt as if I belonged because what I was contributing to golf instruction was, to my mind, groundbreaking. I worked in a number of *Golf Digest* schools and eventually had some of my own.

I was frankly surprised that Snead bought into the idea of

Swing the Handle. Sam and I had developed a relationship that began when we played an exhibition together in 1950 when I was seventeen. We were paired together in the third round at the PGA Championship in Dallas in 1963 with Dow Finsterwald. I played with him one year at Bel-Air, and we were paired together in the PGA Club Pro Championship in Arizona. He came to Bel-Air as our Friends of Golf honoree. Over the years, we became good friends.

He liked the idea of Swing the Handle. Toski, who was perhaps the preeminent teacher of the day, liked the idea as well. Nelson endorsed me as a teacher and was very complimentary of my work.

Every day I played, every day I taught, every time I swung the club I was convinced that Swing the Handle was revolutionary in golf instruction. I never made a swing where I didn't think I was on the right track.

While convincing the publishers and other teachers was relatively easy, convincing students was another thing entirely. Students are not quick to catch on because they are always battling preconceived notions and past habits. That's what you deal with when you teach any student. But when you try to present something totally foreign to what they have read or heard, the task becomes doubly difficult.

As a teacher, you are trying to convey a word message that lodges in the student's mind so he can take that message and transfer it into habit. That's easy to say, but it still has to be mind over matter to overcome the past habit. He must want to make a change and he needs to be convinced that what is being introduced is going to make him play better in a more effective but simpler way. Students won't try something more complicated, but they will try something simpler.

You can't present anything simpler than Swing the Handle. It overrides anything you are trying to do. Most modern golf instruction deals with positions, segments, different moves, different swing planes, different arcs, and that becomes complicated to the point of confusion. The swing itself takes two seconds. The mind cannot comprehend fifteen different thoughts dealing with positions and moves and keys in that blink of an eye.

So you must have something to make the swing comprehensive, knowing what causes the swing to happen. If you can reduce all the technical thought to one thought, that's nirvana. And you can do that with Swing the Handle. Everything you see the ball do is controlled by what you do with the handle of the club. You simply swing the handle with your forearms from one side of the body to the other. What could be simpler?

Fred Astaire

FRED ASTAIRE DIDN'T WALK. HE GLIDED THROUGH THE GRILL ROOM at Bel-Air and his brown suede shoes hardly touched the floor. His days at the club were spent with equal parts grace and charm.

He was always impeccably dressed, always wore an ascot, and if he wore a jacket, there was always a handkerchief in the pocket. He was by all means a gentleman and beautiful to behold.

Astaire was one of the more popular members at Bel-Air. He enjoyed all the members, but he had some favorites— Fred MacMurray, Ray Bolger, Jimmy Stewart—whom he especially liked to play golf with.

As a golfer, he was just as graceful. He had great posture and balance. But he had the average golfer's lament: "Little Pro, how do I get more distance?" That's a most precious commodity for most players.

But he could strike the ball solidly. In one film, he danced up to a row of golf balls and hit them one after another rapid-fire. And he didn't miss a shot.

Astaire wanted to hit the ball farther, like most of us. So I wanted him to employ more forearm strength through the ball. To convey this feeling during our lesson, I put the toe of my right foot on top of his ball and asked him to place his clubface to the back of the ball and push the handle with all his might. He could feel his total body strength emanating within his forearms being employed in this isometric demonstration.

All the while, during this workout, Fred Astaire never perspired, never loosened his silk belt, nor did he remove his ascot. Who of us could do that?

Larry Brown

I HAD A SPEAKING ENGAGEMENT FOR THE PGA OF AMERICA AT THE group's annual teaching summit in 2002 and the topic of my presentation had to do with the difference between coaching and teaching. I asked Larry Brown, who has been a member at Bel-Air for ten years or so, to give me some help with my talk. I wanted to know, from his point of view, what the difference is and which he considers himself to be—a coach or a teacher.

He thinks of himself as a teacher. He enjoys the daily workouts, working with players, trying to help new players become better, trying to help older, more established players get the most out of their abilities and put it all together in the form of a team concept. So when they take the floor in competition, they're prepared to win over a long season of one hundred or more games, including the playoffs.

The difference between teaching and coaching in his eyes is this: "Teaching is the art of training the individual to perform at his uppermost level. Coaching is the opportunity to take a group of players and see what they can do in competition toward the end reward of winning."

I don't know of anyone more qualified to tell the difference than Brown. As coach of the Detroit Pistons, he won the 2004 NBA Championship and was within one game of defending the title, losing to San Antonio in game seven of the NBA Finals in 2005.

Brown has coached all over—Detroit, Philadelphia, Indiana, Denver, San Antonio, and the Los Angeles Clippers in the NBA; Carolina and Denver in the old ABA; UCLA and Kansas in college. He took UCLA to the NCAA Championship final game in 1980 and won the NCAA Championship with Kansas in 1988.

Larry has an unbridled passion for golf, and at this stage of his career, his passion for golf just might exceed his passion for basketball. He likes golf because it is an individual game where you can truly see the fruits of your labor instantly. I've talked a lot of golf with Larry over the years, and he always keeps up with the latest happenings with UCLA players whom I coached there and with PGA Tour players with whom we might share a common interest. He wants to know what they do and how they might do it better.

Brown plays to a 6 handicap and is also a member at the Atlantic Club on Long Island. In between, he plays at every good golf course he can fit into his schedule. He's forever tinkering with his golf swing, never quite satisfied with what he's doing. As with most good players, he's always looking for that little clue that's going to open the next door for him.

As good a teacher as he is, he's an even better student.

Learning Environment

FOR LEARNING TO TAKE PLACE, THE STUDENT must want to learn. That sounds overly simplistic, but it's a notion that's vital. More than once, I've had students say they wanted to learn, but they came armed with so many preconceived notions that what they really wanted was for me to validate their bad habits.

Everyone has problems with his golf swing, even the best players in the world. Which means that everyone needs to get better. In order to do so, he must learn new things about his golf swing. But if you simply are too stubborn to be open-minded enough to learn, no improvement can occur.

Anyone who wants to learn can do so. The good teacher enjoys working with somebody who wants to learn. It's fun and there's no end to it. One thing segues into another. You enter a room and there's a door. You unlock that door and then you go into another room and there's another door. It goes on and on.

As a player, you have dozens, maybe hundreds of questions. As a teacher, you are trying to answer all the questions. The player needs satisfactory answers to every question. Neither of you can afford the unanswered question. That's when you haul off and swing and you look up and you see the ball do something unfamiliar. Then you have that big blank stare on your face. It's a question mark. Your swing did something, causing the ball to do something, and you don't know why.

Once you get those answers and are satisfied with them, you need to categorize them, putting them in the right department so that you know when to draw what from where. It's like organizing your room so that you know where to find things instead of wading through one big mess.

The most difficult people to teach are those who are hard of listening. They want to talk, to argue, and to think of something that's happening elsewhere. They're not really tuned in to what you're saying. The teacher needs somehow to tune them in so he can communicate that mental picture they need.

In the beginning, I had difficulty creating a word picture of Swing the Handle. Even now, most people have heard of Swing the Handle, but they don't know what that means. As simple as the concept is, it still doesn't make an imprint in people's minds. That's when I use the analogy of the two-armed tennis stroke. When I say that to people, they don't envision a golf swing. But they are able to translate that notion of a tennis stroke into their own golf swing. That's learning.

Sean Connery

THE YEAR SEAN CONNERY WON THE ACADEMY AWARD FOR *The Untouchables* was the same year he won another trophy.

Connery is a member of the Royal & Ancient Golf Club at St. Andrews, and each year, the R&A holds a member conclave they call the Silver Jubilee. It's a handicap event and all the attending members are thrown into a bracket and the championship is conducted at match play.

Surprisingly enough, he won the tournament and the BBC broadcast the event all over Great Britain. I believe winning the Silver Jubilee meant more to him than winning the Oscar.

Today, he plays to a 10 handicap, although he was as low as a 6 at one time. He loves to talk about the game and I have given him some lessons. He always was concerned about the different positions of the golf swing. He looked in mirrors and was constantly checking to make certain the club was in the right position. I've always tried to discourage that, emphasizing that the swing is a whole, not the sum of its parts.

If you see a player looking at himself in the mirror or a pane of glass, you know he is position minded. It really becomes a vanity check. What good does it do to check your positions when you are in the middle of a round trying to shoot a score?

You had better be set on what the ball is going to do and how you make it do that. It is much preferable that you have a comprehensive swing thought in mind. The swing is about a three-hundred-degree arc around your body. Every one of those degrees represents a point along that arc.

If you worry about points along that arc, you are going to be like the centipede, wondering which foot to put forward next.

One day, Connery was at Bel-Air and we were in the locker room talking about some aspect of the swing. He had just finished showering, and it dawned upon me that here I was in the locker room with a completely nude Sean Connery.

Probably every woman in the world would like to have been in my shoes at that moment. The Little Pro and a nude James Bond!

Jimmy Connors

WHEN JIMMY CONNORS FIRST CAME HERE TO PLAY IN THE EARLY 1980s, he was still in the twilight of his tennis career. Instead of Connors the brat, he was Jimmy the father and husband, trying to validate himself as one of the greats of the game.

After he got into golf, we were introduced. It occurred to me that as a great athlete, he should be a better golfer. But he really didn't know what the golf swing was all about. He was developing some pretty peculiar habits that would impede his progress if he didn't make some very fundamental changes.

I suggested to him that the golf swing is exactly like the two-handed tennis stroke. When tennis players make such a swing of the racket, they are making a perfect little golf swing. He was the master of such a stroke and I thought it would be a wonderful visual for him to develop a golf swing. Jimmy didn't like that idea. He thought the golf swing was a pulling downward of the left side, which I believe causes all sorts of problems. The two-armed stroke might be good for tennis, he thought, but it wasn't good for golf.

I saw him again in 1997 when he appeared at Bel-Air for the Little Pro Member-Guest, and we renewed our acquaintance. Shortly afterward, he appeared for golf lessons. I made the same suggestions that I had previously, and all of a sudden, it struck home with him. He could see and feel the forearms employed in the golf swing. Now that his swing concept was good, we could start tailoring some of the shots he wanted to hit.

Today, he is a legitimate 4- or 5-handicap player. He has a good work ethic and wants to get better. He can, now that he has the right concept.

The Target

THE GAME IN ITS SIMPLEST SENSE GOES FROM Point A to Point B, from where the ball is to where we want it to go. From the longest drive to the shortest putt, you have to choose a target every time you want to play a shot. From that target, a lot of information comes in the form of distance,  in the form of terrain, whether it's level, uphill, or downhill, whether there's wind. There could be obstacles in the form of trees, there could be hazards or boundaries that come into play. When you size up your target, all this information comes back. It filters through your mental computer.

From that point, you can further evaluate your shot. You might have to take more or less club because the target is significantly uphill or downhill from your ball. You might have to plan to curve the ball away from a hazard or to curve it around an obstacle.

But you should always be mindful of the target. You can't get there if you don't know where you're going. You should be able to shut your eyes and still see the target in your mind's eye. The mind-set is on the target and the target dictates the shot you envision.

The Russians Are Coming

IN THE EARLY 1980S, AFTER TWELVE YEARS OF NEGOTIATIONS, THE Russian government finally agreed to build the country's first regulation eighteen-hole golf course. American industrialist Armand Hammer, who had been instrumental in easing tensions between the United States and the Soviet Union, was key to the golfing diplomacy.

Robert Trent Jones Jr., son of the great golf course architect, would be the designer. Jones invited six Russian engineers to visit some of his golf courses to see firsthand what a course should look like and to give them some idea of how one should be built. Jones met the engineers in New York and they toured the country, inspecting some of the nation's finest courses. They visited Robert Trent Jones Sr.'s handiwork at Hazeltine National in Minneapolis. From there, they traveled to San Francisco to Bohemian Grove and down to Pebble Beach to see creations by Jones Jr. at Spyglass Hill, Poppy Hills, and Spanish Bay.

While in San Francisco, they were treated to a college football game between Stanford and the University of California. It wasn't anything like the football to which they were accustomed. What they think of as football, we call soccer. When offered a hot dog, the Russians were overheard to say, "It isn't really dog!"

Let's see, football that really isn't football and a hot dog that isn't really dog. Talk about culture shock.

The last leg of the journey to Pebble Beach featured an airplane ride over some of America's most beautiful real estate. Bobby had asked me to come up and greet his Russian guests and offer them a golf clinic at Spanish Bay, which is a lovely creation by the triumvirate of Jones, former USGA president Sandy Tatum, and golfing great Tom Watson.

In true Scottish links tradition, there is no practice ground at Spanish Bay. In looking around for a place to conduct the clinic, I spotted the red tee markers on the first tee and thought that spot would be more than appropriate. None of the six engineers had ever swung a golf club. I was in for quite an experience.

The clinic, conducted through an interpreter, went off without a hitch. It ended as the sun was setting on the horizon down behind Bird Rock with me hitting a perfect drive down the first fairway, which heads down to the sea. But that was not the end of the day. Our Russian guests, under the giddy influence of having caught golf fever, insisted on playing the first hole.

Number one at Spanish Bay is a beautiful par 5 with a ridge of sand running down the left side. The Russians looked like ants, crisscrossing the fairway until they approached the green. As is the custom there, a solitary bagpiper plays while walking down the ridge from the clubhouse to the first green. It was there that our Russian friends surrounded the bagpiper and began a spirited conversation.

It seems the piper was a language student in nearby Pacific Grove and spoke fluent Russian. The golf gods could not have created a more perfect scenario. We would need the vodka that was raised in toasts that evening.

Today, the Moscow Golf Club flourishes and these engineers think they invented the game. It is indeed a small world, hopefully a better one.

An Unorthodox Lesson

AT THE *GOLF DIGEST* SCHOOLS, THERE WAS AN exercise that I thought was priceless. The idea was to use the teaching panel to espouse different ideas on a particular subject so that the *Golf Digest* editors could create editorial content on instruction.

The panel consisted of about a dozen teachers and players and we'd get together twice a year. We'd spend three days in places like Orlando and Pinehurst, and they'd lock us in a room where we would bat back and forth prepared questions from the magazine's editors. The questions were meant to be provocative so that this panel of experts could create a contrast, perhaps some controversy, from which they could produce interesting magazine articles.

It was the role of every person at that table to answer the question in his own vernacular, while being tried by a jury of his peers. So you'd best know what you were talking about. It made for a very interesting contrast, and there were a lot of differences of opinion that came out of those question-and-answer sessions. To me, it was a healthy free exchange of ideas, and readers were welcome to find an answer to a question and to determine which answer was best in each particular case.

Once, we sat around a table and the topic came up about how to conduct a playing lesson. Bob Toski answered one way and Jim Flick answered another and John Jacobs had something else entirely. Then it came time for Sam Snead to answer. He said, "The best playing lesson is without a ball."

We all stopped with our mouths wide open, wondering what in the world he meant. He explained: You take a student out on the golf course and move him from station to station, from the tee to a place in the fairway where he might have hit his tee shot. From that point, he imagines what his next shot into the green is to be. Then the student would make an imaginary swing without the ball and he'd imagine it behaving precisely as he wanted. He'd march the student down near the green and stand him in the heavy grass with the idea that he had a pitch shot that he needed to get into the air and stop in a hurry. The player would take an imaginary swing and see the ball come to rest a couple of feet from the hole.

By taking the ball out of play, Snead contended, the trauma for the student of having to watch a lousy shot was removed. Because most people react negatively to a poor shot, the attitude for the next shot increases exponentially. I thought it was a brilliant way to treat the playing lesson and I've used the same kind of idea myself from time to time. Thanks, Sam!

It's really the idea of what a practice swing should be about. When you make a practice swing, include all the ingredients that you need in a real shot. Key on a specific spot where you want the club to brush the ground. Have your mind set on a certain target and link those two—Point A and Point B—and have your mind's eye picture what you want the ball to do.

Every golf shot that we play is a problem to be solved. You assess all the information that comes into play with the ball and the target, and you select a club with which to play that shot. Then you envision the shot to be played.

Picture the flight of the ball doing precisely what you want it to do relative to the target you have in mind. Whether you prefer a draw or a fade, the one that is more comfortable to you gives you more confidence when you are preparing to hit the shot. And it's easier to picture the ball in flight doing what you are most confident producing.

Now you've programmed the shot. You've assessed the lie and defined your target and pictured the solution in the form of a target. When you picture the shot, you tap into that most creative part of you. The most expert golf players in the game are able to see in their mind's eye exactly what they want the ball to do. And when they are able to see it that clearly, the ability to put the swing into motion to create what they see becomes even more natural. Especially so if you swing the handle according to this picture.

Hugh Grant

STANDING ON THE PUTTING GREEN, HUGH GRANT CREATED QUITE a stir. It was ladies' day at Bel-Air, and a number of women were in the grill room that overlooks the putting green. Two of the club's female employees were standing nearby, hoping for an introduction. It is one of the hazards a man of his looks and fame has to face. We should all have it so tough.

I met Hugh during the week of the Academy Awards one year, and I got the impression that he was a fairly new golfer. It was suggested that he come have a lesson with me. We worked for three days or so, spending about two hours a day on the practice tee. He enjoyed it because he was showing some progress, and I enjoyed it because he was getting my concepts about the golf swing, a three-dimensional concept that he could take with him.

I believe that the golf swing is three-dimensional, but it is taught as anything but. If you listen to people describe their swing, they usually put themselves into one of three categories:

1. The player who wants to get his hands as high as possible with an up-to-down motion

2. The player who takes the club back, moves into the ball, and extends through, creating width

3. The player who wants to turn to the right going back and turn to the left coming through, creating depth

Which one is right? All three. But they are all incomplete because a good golf swing does all of the above—it's high, wide, and deep. That is too much to think of at once, but you do need to be fully aware of each, or you'll never fully appreciate the concept of your swing.

On the last day we worked together, on the day after the

Academy Awards, he told me he had to leave, that he was on his way to propose marriage to Sandra Bullock. I have no idea what happened and, of course, I haven't seen him since.

But I hope his golf game has worked out a little better.

Uncomplicated Minds

BESIDES LITTLE CHILDREN, PROBABLY THE easiest people to teach are those who have never played the game. It's important to get to them before they get preconceived notions that turn into physical habits. People with ingrained habits resist new information because of the conflict between  the thought and the habit. They tend to resist and reject what you are trying to teach them, so there has to be a belief that what you are teaching will work for them so it becomes mind over matter.

You can retrain the muscles, but psychologists will tell you that to get rid of an ingrained habit and replace it with a new thought that will eventually become an instinctive reaction takes about twenty-eight days, if practiced every day. It takes constant repetition for such learning to take place.

The simple act of picking up a fork and putting a morsel of food in your mouth is instinctive to you. But if you had never done it and were attempting to train to feed yourself with a fork, you'd be apt to poke yourself in the eye or miss your mouth for twenty-eight days until it became a subconscious reaction.

So if such a simple act can be difficult, then certainly swinging the golf club is exponentially more difficult. Re-training the muscle system is not easy.

That's why when it's all said and done, the student needs a comprehensive idea. Swing the Handle is the key to that idea. It's very important that golf players have a consistent swing concept. What I mean by the swing concept is that a player must see in his mind's eye what a good golf swing looks like. Everyone knows what a good baseball swing looks like. More simply, everyone knows how to throw a ball. You don't have to emulate Derek Jeter to know how to throw. The same thing applies to tennis or football or any game with a ball.

But in the mind of a golfer, all kinds of strange pictures occur. Usually those pictures change from day to day, month to month. How can you expect there to be progress in golf if there isn't a continuity of thought and a consistency of action as a result of that? So, yes, it is imperative that a golfer have in mind what the swing is.

But what is it? If you threw that question out there for a panel of one hundred so-called experts, you'd be amazed at the different answers you'd get. If there's not a consistency of thought among the panel of experts, how in the world can there be a consistency of thought with the players? If a concept is conveyed that makes some sense and can resonate in the thinking of a player, then that's a big help toward his progress as a golfer.

If I had to describe what a golf swing is to try to lodge that in somebody's head, I'd say it's strictly a swinging motion from one side of the body to the other, created by the forearms, swinging the handle end of the club. So that's the concept—you're swinging the handle of the club from one side of the body to the other side of the body. If you want to be more specific than that, you swing it over each hip, over the right hip in the backswing, over the left hip in the forward swing. That is the mental concept that I'd want a player to go with. Then I can help answer the other questions that are bound to pop up.

I did a teaching seminar in Las Vegas for the PGA of America in 1999 at the request of Education Chairman Ralph Bernhisel, and I asked the question before the lecture: What is playing the game? Even the best teachers in the world all have different concepts about playing the game. Some emphasize the physical aspects of playing, some emphasize the mental aspects. Some talk about discipline, others talk about freedom.

I asked the same question regarding the golf swing. Once again, these best golf instructors in the world couldn't reach a consensus about how the golf club should be swung. If they are not in concert, how can we as teachers communicate consistent ideas to students? Consistency is made up of repetition. You must have a consistent swing concept and you must repeat it enough times that it breeds confidence.

Ray Bolger

ONE OF THE CHARMS OF BEL-AIR IS THAT CELEBRITIES HAVE A place to play golf and enjoy some fellowship away from the spotlight of fame. There are so many famous people at the club that no one person really stands out. There aren't many places they can go where they are assured of anonymity. At Bel-Air, each member respects the club as a haven from the pressures and demands of the world of celebrity.

We have club rules against photography and it's against the rules for guests to ask members for autographs. We try to respect the members' privacy.

From time to time, however, some members are called on to do things for the club. Ray Bolger was one of those people. He was the pride of Bel-Air and was almost universally liked and admired. If we needed a celebrity to appear at a tournament or get up and say a few things at a club event, Bolger never hesitated. He was always willing. As long as he felt appreciated, he'd go on forever.

He was entertaining on and off the course. He was a joy to play with. He loved to talk with people of all stripes. He could meet a rank stranger or a guest of the club and engage that person in conversation. As long as he felt welcome, he'd welcome the other person. He had a style and grace about him along with a wonderful sense of humor. No one was a better storyteller. He was much more than just the scarecrow in *The Wizard of Oz*.

As a golfer, Bolger was well above average. He probably

got down to a 9 handicap at one time, but for the most part, his handicap hovered around 13 or 14. He loved to play in the big pro-ams, particularly the Hope and the Crosby. In fact, he once played in an exhibition at Merion with former President Eisenhower and Arnold Palmer.

I never formally taught Bolger, but he was famous for getting what we call "bootleg" lessons. That's a term we use for a lesson on the go. We'd be out playing and he would pump me for tips during the round. That's not always the best way to patch up an ailing golf game, but it worked for him.

Mac Davis

NOT MANY PEOPLE KNOW THAT MAC DAVIS IS A SUCCESSFUL Broadway actor, having appeared in a long-running production of Pierre Cossette's *Will Rogers Follies*. Most know him for his singing and his television variety show in the 1970s. And some remember his role in the movie *North Dallas Forty*.

I know him for his golf and his always congenial demeanor when he comes to play at Bel-Air. He's a legitimate 6-handicap player, and when he's in town, he plays six days a week. Everybody has to take one day off, and Mac's day is Sunday. If he's not working on a project, you will find him here playing golf.

He is never satisfied, and you could call him a perfectionist. But he's also a realist and he knows he will never achieve perfection in an imperfect game. If he doesn't hit it quite right, he might complain, but in truth, he enjoys the pursuit. He always knows it could be better. Tiger Woods isn't satisfied, either, but he keeps it to himself better than Mac does.

He's a good swinger and he's been around Bel-Air as low as 68. A day out of the 70s is a bad day for Mac. He was in my *Swing the Handle* video series and even sang me a little song in Volume III, "Shotmaking Procedure."

He's quite popular among the caddies at Bel-Air, and every year at the caddie dinner, he makes up a song, calling each caddie by name. It's impressive that he remembers all the caddies and it's certain they will all remember him.

Advanced Students

YOU'D THINK THAT PGA TOUR PLAYERS WOULD BE DIFFICULT TO teach, but they're really not. Tour players are easy to teach in the sense that when you are dealing with a more progressed student, you have the job of fine-tuning the player. Whereas with beginning players, you are trying to create a swing and the good habits that go with it.

Tour players tend to want to talk about finer points that have to do with cause and effect, certain kinds of sophisticated shots they hit, perhaps a treatment of rhythm and tempo. It's not a matter of changing fundamentals or their basic swing. They've pretty much figured out how they want to set up and how they want to swing. It's the subtleties that make the difference to the Tour player.

Or it could be how he relates to the target. Does he have all his bases covered? There are four bases to cover when it comes to dealing with the target. First you have to deal with the ball and how it lies. Then you have to relate to the target and how you want to set your club and your body. Third, you picture the shot and how it is to be shaped. Finally, you have the swing thought to set things in motion.

Beyond that, with a Tour player, you get into the science of playing the game of golf, whereby you set his mind straight regarding what his real goals are versus what the rewards are or what his target might be. There's a difference between targeting something that might happen in the near or distant future—a major championship on the horizon—versus a goal, which is more nearly obtainable.

For instance, if a Tour player is competing in an event that leads up to a major championship, his focus might be too far into the future, like preparing for the major. Instead, his focus needs to be on the goal at hand—the shot he is playing, the hole he is playing, the round he is playing, and the tournament he is playing.

The reward for those goals consists of the quality of the shot, the relation to par on a hole or in a round, and the relation of the round as it pertains to the 72-hole tournament.

Those are the kinds of things I would talk to a Tour player about, but it all goes back to the questions he is asking. He doesn't want my entire pharmacy, just the remedy for his particular problem.

Craig T. Nelson

HERE'S ALL YOU NEED TO KNOW ABOUT CRAIG NELSON: FOR ONE, he once took the entire crew of the television series in which he starred, *The District,* to Pebble Beach for a golf holiday. Second, we were having lunch in the grill room at Bel-Air, and you have to understand that the room is full of captains of industry and entertainment. Not many tend to be religious at all. But as Craig and I sat down to dine, he said a little prayer before taking a bite of food. I don't think I had witnessed that before or since.

Craig appeared in the *Swing the Handle* video in Volume I, "Fundamentals." He demonstrates the fundamentals very well. In a subsequent lesson, he was intrigued to learn the important role that the elbows play in developing a sound, repeating golf swing. I explained to him that in order for the shoulders and hips to rotate on a level plane, the elbows must also remain level as they move from side to side.

The drill that helped him understand this movement called for Nelson to hold his elbows in the palms of his hands while assuming the address position in the setup. I then had him swing his elbows from right to left without allowing them to bob up and down. He got the message and his golf swing is much more consistently "on plane."

Craig Nelson is superb in all of his acting roles. His success in *Coach, The District, The Incredibles,* and others is simply a portent of things to come. His strength of character and his love of family, friends, and country manifest vividly in his acting as well as his golf game!

A low-handicap player at Bel-Air and Sherwood, Craig T. Nelson loves to compete. He is a regular performer at the AT&T tournament and other high-level pro-ams. His personality makes him popular with the galleries.

I know him in a variety of roles. The one I like best was his voice-over effort in my son Michael's James Dean film, *Little Bastard*. After the "takes," Craig T. and I had our elbow golf lesson at the Bel-Air Hotel. The curious hotel guests could not deter us.

Goals

GOLF IS ONE OF THE ONLY GAMES THAT PEOPLE begin at any age and can play as long as they can swing a club. But most people have no idea how to approach the playing of the game. We form all kinds of impressions about golf, usually off the mark. We think that enjoyment of the game depends  on our performance, but we have no idea how to maximize our performance.

That's where goals come into play. People actually mix up goals with the rewards that come from chasing the goals. For instance, a goal is to hit a shot as well as we possibly can. The reward is the result of that shot, good or bad. A goal is to play the hole in relation to par as well as we possibly can. The reward is the score on the hole—birdie, par, bogey. A goal is to play the eighteen-hole round in relation to par as well as we possibly can. The reward is the score at the end of the day, satisfying or not.

Ken Venturi

FROM THE TIME OF HIS BIRTH, KEN VENTURI HAS BEEN DEFYING the odds. As a child and into young manhood, Kenny had a stuttering problem.

Not only did he overcome this speech impediment, he went on to become one of the foremost golf telecasters of the twentieth century.

Ken became, due to his determination and work ethic, not only a survivor but a true champion as a junior, amateur, and professional golfer. Highlighting this impressive career was his monumental victory in the U.S. Open at Congressional in 1964.

Frank Chirkinian of CBS Television offered Venturi the opportunity to go into broadcasting in the late '60s. This made for a thirty-five-year career whereby Ken Venturi became a golfing household word. Negative became a definite positive as he used his stuttering days as incentive to achieve.

A native of San Francisco and a product of Harding Park, where his dad was manager, Ken has strong reverence for this great old facility, which has recently been renovated to become a true championship venue for the future. He played in the finals of the Hearst National Junior, and won the San Francisco City and California State Amateur Championships while representing Harding Park. He was named to the 1953 Walker Cup team while schooling at nearby San Jose State.

Some fourteen tour victories came after turning pro in 1956 following his "near miss" at the Masters wherein an 80 in the last round made Jack Burke Jr. a 1-stroke winner. The last victory came in the San Francisco Open at the same Harding Park where Ken began his golfing journey. Akin to the salmon returning upstream after a swim out to sea, Venturi came home to settle.

The twilight of Ken Venturi's career has been spent with friends, family, and loved ones in Florida, Palm Springs, San Francisco, and Bel-Air, where he is an honorary member. His U.S. Open trophy and his Presidents Cup replica are proudly housed at Bel-Air.

It has been a true pleasure to see him rebound from the loss of his adored wife, Beau, and then see him find happiness with his new wife, Kathleen. His devotion to charity efforts and worthy causes has won him praises all over. He even found time to dabble in teaching and club design work. Ken Venturi's is a great success story!

College Coach

I BECAME THE MEN'S GOLF COACH AT UCLA IN 1975 AND remained in that post for fourteen years. The previous coach was Vic Kelley, who had been coaching the team since the late 1940s. He was a wonderful man and was president of the Golf Coaches Association of America, but he was not a full-time coach. He was also the sports information director at the university and was limited in his resources involving the team.

He approached me in 1973 about taking over the Bruins, and I took the proposal to our board at Bel-Air. They thought I shouldn't do it, that it would be a conflict of interest. A couple of years later, Charles Young, the UCLA chancellor, became a member at Bel-Air, and he asked me if I would become the golf coach. He couldn't understand why the golf program at UCLA seemed to be the weakest link in the whole athletic department.

I went back to the board, and this time I was granted permission to coach the team. It was a great challenge to take a program that had suffered over the years and see if we could do something with it and succeed. It was also an opportunity to test my teaching ability with a group of young players who were scratch caliber and find out if we could compete.

But then the work actually began. We had to get golf courses to play, we had to raise money to support the program, we had to improve the schedule, and we had to recruit the athletes. We needed the right players and to train them correctly so they would be prepared to go out into competition.

The challenge was fun, and we had a sense of pride and accomplishment when the results came in. We had a ten-year run during which we won an NCAA championship, fifty-seven team tournaments, and twenty-five individual titles, and had two players—Corey Pavin in '82 and Duffy Waldorf in '85—voted college player of the year. We had sixteen All-American players and we have had eight UCLA players competing on the PGA Tour.

I'd say we did pretty well.

Top Recruits

ONE OF THE BEST PLAYERS IN UCLA HISTORY IS DUFFY WALDORF, whom I've known since he was seventeen years old. He worked with me as a junior player and I was able to recruit him to the school. We had a lot of success together. He was a first team All-American and went on to make the Walker Cup team.

Since he turned professional, he's won four PGA Tour events and has contended in major championships. All he needs is a little more intent to win and there's no telling what he might do.

Beyond his ability as a golf player, he's a wonderful human being whose priorities are in the right place. He is devoted to his family and friends, and golf probably ranks third in line.

To Duffy, those things are much more important than pursuing golf tournament titles. He believes, and perhaps rightly so, that what he has accomplished in his relationships with family and friends will be far more meaningful in his life.

Steve Pate was one of my main recruits in 1979, and he ended up justifying the faith I had in him. He was a first team All-American in 1983 and went on to do great things in professional golf. He made the Ryder Cup twice, finished third in the U.S. Open and third in the Masters, and was in the final pair at the 1992 British Open at Muirfield.

His swing is not the most classic you have ever seen, but he has great rhythm and is a wonderful putter, one of the best on the PGA Tour. When he gets a hot hand, it's almost embarrassing how many putts he makes. He once made seven birdies in a row at the Masters.

Pate played a vital role in the United States' victory in the 1999 Ryder Cup at Brookline. He won his singles match and partnered with Tiger Woods to win a critical four-ball match.

He is known for his temperamental outbursts and is nick-named "Volcano" on the tour. Early in his career, he'd tend to let his emotions get the better of him on the spot. He later learned to harness that energy to better things.

It's all right to care about the shot you just played. Just don't care too much.

Richard Crenna

ONE OF MY FONDEST MEMORIES CAME WITH RICHARD CRENNA by my side. We were partners in the Bing Crosby Pro-Am in 1965 and we came to the par-3 seventh hole, the biggest little hole in the world. It measures only about 110 yards, and on a normal day, a sand wedge will get the job done. But on this day, the wind was howling in from Carmel Bay. The wind was blowing so strongly that I saw touring professionals take 4-irons and watch their shots peel off like a seagull and fall into the sea.

We were standing on the tee waiting for the group ahead to clear, trying to figure out what to do. Richard said, "Little Pro, whatever club you take, pipe it in there." I took a 3-iron and played a glorified chip shot. The ball traveled down the hill, never got up, and headed on a straight line, like a martin to its gourd. The flagstick was in the back right corner and the ball rolled like a rat to its hole right into the cup. That was to be my claim to fame after fifteen years of playing in the Crosby.

Richard was an avid golfer, and his swing reminded me of an old upright piano. His was an up-and-down swing with no depth to it. But he was determined that his was the old classic swing and was right for him.

When we had lessons, I'd ask him if we were going to rehearse the upright swing. He was insistent; he liked what he was doing. You can't teach someone something he doesn't want to learn. So we had to take whatever he had in mind and learn to live with it. It became my job to try to teach him some shots to hit using what he came equipped with.

With every student, you have to sense what he can receive and how much he can absorb. Some can absorb quite a bit and some can't absorb very much at all. As a teacher, you are trying to answer questions and arrest problems.

There are a lot of ways to convey a message. You can do it verbally, you can describe a mental picture, you can use the written word, or you can do it by demonstration, taking him by the hand and moving him physically through the swing.

Crenna and I once did a piece for *Golf Magazine* near the eighteenth green at Bel-Air on bunker shots. He hadn't been a good bunker player and was having a difficult time. I suggested that concentrating on a single grain of sand with the idea of getting that grain near the hole is much too hard. But if you look at that one grain and swing hundreds of grains out, the one you have in mind comes out with the rest.

You should treat the ball the same way. It does no good to look behind the ball. Treat the ball like one large grain of sand. Swing lots of sand out and the ball comes out with the sand.

From Short-Range to Long-Long-Range

THERE ARE FOUR GOALS OF A STROKE-PLAY event: short-range, medium-range, long-range, and long-long-range. The short-range goal is to play the shot facing you, staying in the moment and taking each shot as it comes. The medium-range goal is to relate to par as well as you possibly  can on each hole, instead of awarding yourself scores you haven't yet made.

You see PGA Tour players come to par-5 holes and their mouths water at the prospect of the birdie or eagle they are certain they will make, only to be disappointed when they come away with a 5 or 6 on the hole. It's like a child looking in the window of a candy store, wanting to get his hands on all the goodies. He doesn't realize he has to take certain steps to get inside the store.

In a stroke-play event, how do you manage your game to get you to the reward? You play shot by shot, hole by hole, giving each its proper respect. How are you going to manage your game for the total round? That's the long-term goal.

In a match-play situation, it's a matter of survival. You have to win more holes than your opponent, or the tournament is over for you. In some cases, that sense of survival becomes so great that you begin to play over your head. But what about stroke play? Let's borrow a page from match play. Old Man Par becomes your opponent. When you have that attitude, you become more conservative in your shot making. Out of necessity, you learn at some point when to lay up instead of trying to play a miracle shot. Don't take foolish chances; strokes are hard to come by.

The next goal, the long-long-term goal, is the four-round tournament. If you exercise the first three goals well, you've done all you can possibly do that week. Maybe you are rewarded by winning!

Greg Norman

THE TRUE MEASURE OF A SUPERSTAR IS HIS PROPENSITY FOR giving back to the game that has been so good to him. In that regard, Greg Norman stands with the elite. There is only one club in America that has in its possession replicas of the trophies of all four major championships and the Ryder Cup. We have those trophies at Bel-Air.

The Claret Jug that symbolizes the winner of the British Open—called the Open Championship in Great Britain—was won twice by Norman. And one of his replica trophies resides in our trophy case. After he won his second British Open at Royal St. George's in 1993, the board of directors of Bel-Air voted to accord him honorary membership for his contributions to the game and to Bel-Air. He then offered his trophy to be housed here.

Greg met Ron Waranch, a member at Bel-Air, in the early '80s, and they began to spend a lot of time together. He played here fairly often in his bachelor days. He had returned to Bel-Air for Waranch's wedding and by then had participated in our Friends of Golf outing.

During that time, Norman was in the midst of a ten-year span in which he was the favorite in all forty majors in which he participated. He won two, but it is widely felt that he should have won four or five more. In my opinion, he never figured out the psychology that goes with winning. You don't win golf tournaments by trying to win golf tournaments. Winning is a reward for playing individual shots, individual holes, and individual rounds while relating to par the best you can. Winning is a reward, not a goal.

Greg was our Friends of Golf honoree in 1988, and for the outing, we paired Norman and Bob Knight, then the coach of the University of Indiana basketball team. Knight's team had just won the NCAA Championship.

It was truly a meeting of the champions, but in our estimation none stands taller as a person than does Greg Norman.

Turning Point

THE BIGGEST CHALLENGE WAS TO LIVE DOWN OUR REPUTATION OF mediocrity at UCLA. Then we had to prove that we could compete with Goliath and chop them down to size, like David did. We were the new boys on the block. We had something to prove, and the only way we could prove it was by winning. But you don't win stake races with claiming horses. So we needed to get the right players, and it took a couple of years.

It was frustrating in the beginning to try and recruit players like Bobby Clampett, Mark O'Meara, John Cook, and others I approached. Nick Faldo, Sandy Lyle, and players of that ilk appreciated what I had to say, but they wanted to go where there was a winning program. We had not yet proved ourselves, which made recruiting all the more difficult.

All of a sudden, a skinny little boy named Corey Pavin came into view. He made a commitment to attend UCLA in his senior year in high school, but we were going to give him only a partial scholarship; we weren't going to risk a full scholarship on an untested commodity. But the summer before he enrolled at UCLA, he went to the semifinals of the U.S. Junior, he won the Junior World in San Diego, he won the Los Angeles City Amateur, and he won a big local junior tournament.

Based on that performance, we gave him the full scholarship that he had earned. He made some swing changes in his freshman year, and toward the end of that year he began to play really well. But as a sophomore, he truly blossomed. He won six tournaments, more than anyone in college golf that year. He made the Walker Cup team and was a first team All-American. A couple of years later, in his senior year, he was college player of the year.

He proved to the other guys on the team that they could win. Corey was a winner, and winners are not content to do anything but win. If you have someone like that in your midst, it rubs off on the others. They looked at a little guy who weighed no more than 140 pounds who was beating big, strong guys simply with heart and brains. They figured that if he could do it, they could.

So he raised the bar. We began to attract better players to UCLA because he started getting a reputation of being a winner. Pavin's success had a great deal to do with that.

But with success comes another new set of challenges. We now had to begin to manage the talent once the good players came to us so they could have the best possible environment in which to get the utmost out of their abilities. That doesn't always happen. Sometimes a heralded player comes to school and begins to live in the past. He's surrounded by players who are just as good as or even better than he is and finds he has to work harder than ever just to stay even with his teammates.

Along the way, we tried to teach them much more than swinging the club. We tried to help them understand the nature of the game and the fact that it's a gentlemen's game. We had a dress code—we wore jackets and ties on the road—and we stressed that they conduct themselves properly because they were representing the university. Not only that, but we were guests of private clubs in the Los Angeles area, and we tried to make the players understand that this was a privilege and not a right.

That attitude, both in dress and manner, was not always popular among the players. But I insisted on it. When we, as a team, walked on an airplane, the passengers couldn't tell what sport we played. But they were impressed with where we came from and who we were. It reflected nicely on the players and the university.

Once, the players managed to get their revenge. In 1979, we had some pretty cantankerous and playful guys on the team. Pavin, Pate, Jay Delsing, Tom Pernice, and Tom Randolph—who now works for NBC—were members of that group.

There was a restaurant outside Tucson that the players liked to frequent, and unbeknownst to me, the custom was that if you entered the restaurant wearing a necktie, the proprietor would take a pair of scissors and snip it off. The players knew a good scheme when they saw it and set a trap for me because I always wore a tie. When we went in, sure enough, he came along and cut my tie off right at the knot.

Luckily, it wasn't my favorite tie. I had a spare for emergencies—like this.

Fred Couples

BEING A COLLEGE GOLF COACH NOT ONLY MEANT THAT I WITNESSED the fine work of my players, but I was fortunate enough to see some of the best young players in the world compete on a national level. Fred Couples was one of the most talented golf players ever to come along.

At one point in his college career, he thought of transferring from Houston to UCLA because he had forged some friendships with the UCLA players. He thought better and, for the sake of loyalty, he finished his career at Houston.

He is a former Masters champion and is one of the great shot makers of our time. He always makes solid contact on every shot. He might be off-line, but he never mishits a shot. More than that, he is one of the most popular players of all time, with fans and peers alike. He's handsome and graceful, and has an air about him that most people find attractive.

I watched him improvise one of the best shots I've ever seen. He was behind the ninth green at the Atlanta Athletic Club, preparing for the PGA Championship. He had hit his approach shot through the green into a bunker in his practice round, and the flagstick was close to the back of the green. The green was elevated toward the back and he had absolutely no shot. He had no green with which to play and his options seemed slim to none.

I was curious to see what he was going to do. He took the edge of his wedge, like you might do on the putting green, and putted the ball up the face of the bunker and through the lip. The ball bounded into the air, came down softly onto the green, and came to rest within 2 feet of the hole.

I would never have dreamed to play such a shot. That's the difference between them and us, I suppose.

Rewards

AFTER THE PURSUIT OF EACH GOAL, THERE IS an appropriate reward. Whatever you score on the hole is your just reward. Whether it's a birdie, par, bogey, or worse, the score is your reward. If you have paid attention to the first two goals, you will have done the best you could on that hole in relation to par.

The lower scores bring a smile to your face, and even a bogey could produce a smile if, in fact, you have avoided a disaster that could have forced your score even higher. If you attend to the things over which you have control, like playing each shot as it comes, you can even get lost in your round and forget what your total score is until you've added it up at the end.

Many times, when a club handicap player is into the round of his life and starts adding up his score before the round is over, he causes a wreck. Up until that moment, he has played the shots and related to par as well as he could and is having a career round. But that cocoon of concentration is broken and he starts to add up his score and he loses it.

You don't win trying to win. We all dream of winning, but we have to focus on the things we can do something about—the four goals. You get what you shoot, but how do you shoot it? By paying attention to the goals. Winning comes as a result. It is the ultimate reward!

Tom Harmon

THE LEGENDARY TOM HARMON WON THE HEISMAN TROPHY IN 1940 for his outstanding play at the University of Michigan. The primary love of his life was his wife, Elyse, an actress he met in Los Angeles. When they married, her wedding gown was made of the material from his parachute that he used when he was shot down over China and rescued there by a missionary.

But the second great love of his life was golf. Harmon had played for a while with the Los Angeles Rams and then got into sports broadcasting. During that broadcasting career, he became a fan of Ben Hogan when he worked on a documentary of his life for a series called *The Legends*.

Harmon was a director for our Friends of Golf organization at Bel-Air, and in one of our meetings, he seized the floor and presented the idea that we should establish a trophy for the amateur golfer of the year. In the process, he wanted the permanent trophy to reside at Bel-Air. To boot, he thought that Hogan's name should be on the trophy. It was the only name that would satisfy him.

Those of us who knew Hogan also knew that he didn't attach his name to things like that. Besides, the Friends of Golf honored college and high school golfers and was not in the business of establishing the top amateur player of the year. Byron Nelson had been one of our Friends of Golf honorees and he helped coach the North Texas State golf team from 1949 to 1952; the team won the NCAA Championship each year. Nelson would have been a perfect choice to have his name on the trophy.

But Harmon would not be fazed. It was Hogan or nothing. So he went off to Fort Worth and persuaded Hogan to participate, an amazing feat in itself. Harmon designed the trophy and commissioned Waterford Crystal to produce it. I'm certain what he had in mind was to create the Heisman Trophy of golf.

That is not, however, how it started. We had to get the College Golf Coaches Association involved and secure its blessing. There were already two awards for the top college player, one named for Jack Nicklaus and the other for Fred Haskins. So we decided to present the award to the All-American academic player of the year. Kevin Wentworth of Oklahoma State won the first one in 1990.

As the years passed, we created a Byron Nelson Award for the outstanding academic player, and the Hogan Award is now for the top amateur player who is still in college. As it turned out, the award became just what Harmon wanted— the Heisman of college golf.

Celine Dion

I WAS ONCE INVITED BY CELINE DION TO ONE OF HER CONCERTS at the Forum in Los Angeles. I took my *Swing the Handle* book to give to her as a gift. Lisa and I were invited backstage before the performance, fifteen minutes before she was to go on. Her husband and manager, René Angélil, waved Lisa and me over, and I presented her with the book.

The next thing I knew, we were having a golf lesson right before she went onstage. Leads one to wonder what she was thinking about when she sang the first song of the concert.

As a result of our meeting, I made a request of her before the 1999 Ryder Cup on behalf of American captain Ben Crenshaw. He wanted her to sing at a concert for the two teams in Boston before the Ryder Cup. She agreed and was perfect.

Celine is quite a golfer, and she has visited Bel-Air on a few occasions with René, who plays golf as well. They own a course in Canada, called Le Mirage, in Terrebonne near Montreal.

She has a pretty classic swing and is a legitimate 18-handicap player. She doesn't hit it out of sight, but she hits it far enough. She's not overpowering, but she consistently moves the ball forward. Most golfers can go up, down, and sideways but not necessarily forward.

She's a fun companion to play with. But you know she's a typical golfer in that she wanted to know all I knew about Swing the Handle in the ten minutes we had backstage together. Here's what I told her:

Most people try to swing the clubhead. I continually use an analogy to tennis to try to communicate my thoughts about the golf swing. I do that because I think it makes the most sense.

I contend that if you focus on the handle of the club, you

cause your body to perform the right motions and indirectly you swing the clubhead. If you give someone a tennis racket, he instinctively knows what to do with it. He swings the handle and the head of the racket follows.

A golf club has the same elements—the grip, the shaft, and the head. You see and feel the head of the club and think you have to hit the ball with that end of the club. It doesn't occur to you that you are making the handle reverse from one side of the body to the other.

If you draw attention to the handle of the club, the head will do what it's meant to do.

Coaching Challenges

IT CAN BE DIFFICULT TO KEEP COLLEGE-AGE PLAYERS IN THE right frame of mind. It's very easy for them to become overconfident, which is almost as bad as not being confident enough. The right emotional level is one of confident apprehension. What I mean by that is you need to be confident enough to believe you are just as good as anyone in the field. But you have to be apprehensive enough to know what lurks, not to take unnecessary chances that can ruin a round.

It's like walking across a darkened room. You don't know what you're going to stumble over next. You know you can walk across the room, but you're careful not to break your neck. As soon as you become overconfident and walk across the room without caution, you trip over something and break your arm.

To try to arrive at the level of confident apprehension and maintain it can be tricky. In any sport, when coaches sense their team is taking something for granted or they're over-confident or cocky, they know a wreck is about to happen, but they can't reverse the trend. You want to try to stop it before it gets to an irreversible point, because if there's an apex, things get away from you.

You want to raise the confidence level to a point just below the apex. If you get above it, it's a long slide before you stop on the way down.

College players are still teachable, if they want to learn. Some will soak up what you have to say and some are hard of hearing. Still others are not good students, they just don't listen very well. They might be instinctively good players, but they're not good students. It's a rare person who is a good student and a good player.

We had a mandatory team meeting once a week. I might conduct that meeting or I might have a guest speaker. The players also were required to have a weekly lesson with me that might last from thirty minutes to an hour. It gave me a chance to find out what they were thinking and what things they were working on in their swings. And I had a chance to convey my own ideas to them.

I also required the players to run at least a mile a day. The norm is to walk eighteen holes, and I wanted them to do something beyond the ordinary. They were always in good shape to play. They had to play at least three rounds a week, and we recorded every score, even the practice scores, so there was no such thing as goofing off.

We had what we called the "differential book," in which we recorded our version of the course rating of the course we played against the player's score. For instance, Bel-Air has a course rating of 72. But on a cold, windy day, we might make the course rating 74. Conversely, if we were playing an easy course with a rating of 71, we might make the rating 68. We would record the players' scores against our adjusted course rating and everyone knew where he stood.

Mark O'Meara

I TRIED TO GET O'MEARA TO COME TO UCLA IN 1977, BUT HE opted to go to Long Beach State, which was closer to his home. He won the 1979 U.S. Amateur, defeating the defending champion, John Cook.

He went on to become a fine professional, winning the Masters and the British Open in 1998. He always had a beautiful sense of rhythm, and thanks to Hank Haney, O'Meara has been bred with a great deal of confidence, both in his technical game and in his putting, of which he was one of the best.

His friendly nature led him to a long-lasting relationship with Tiger Woods. He served as a big brother to Tiger through Woods's formative years and, as a result, I think it actually caused Mark to be a better player. When O'Meara won two majors in 1998, I believe Tiger got some of the credit. They played practice rounds together on the Tour and casual rounds at home in Orlando, and if you are in the company of the best player in the world, some of it is bound to rub off.

Driving

THE PURPOSE OF THE DRIVE IS TO POSITION the ball for the best possible place from which to play the next shot. Plan your shot according to the conditions that prevail. Let your game and the situation determine which kind of shot is best to play.

For instance, imagine a 365-yard par-4 hole with a creek meandering down the left side and a fairway bunker on the right. If you hit the ball 200 yards or more down the left side, the creek comes into play. If you are playing well at the time, you might consider a 3-iron off the tee to an advantageous position where you might have a 7-iron or an 8-iron into the green.

If you aren't playing so well and you feel bold, you might gamble a bit with a driver, and if you are successful, you might have a wedge or less into the green, which might lead to a birdie opportunity.

You must take the hole's design into consideration as well.

The creek feature coming into play off the tee influences your decision. You might not want to take the chance of finding the creek with your ball and bringing bogey or worse into the equation. So the more conservative option takes precedence. But if you are a good, straight driver, you might not give the creek a second thought. Having made your club selection, picture the shot you have in mind and swing the handle over each hip as positively as you can according to that picture.

Glen Campbell

GLEN WAS AN UNDERRATED MUSICIAN. IN HIS EARLY DAYS, HE was a great arranger and worked as a backup musician for a number of artists. Not many people remember that he was a member of the Beach Boys for a while.

I first met him at the Bogey Busters tournament in Dayton, Ohio, an event run by a man named Cy Laughter. Each year, he had a collection of people from government, business, and sports. You might find yourself at dinner with an astronaut, someone like Ray Nietzke of the Green Bay Packers, George H. W. Bush, or Byron Nelson—or all of the above. At the dinner, Laughter would present a customary red jacket to the luminaries who attended.

Byron and I, along with Max Elbin of the PGA of America, were the three golf pros who were invited. John Pike was a Bel-Air member who knew Glen Campbell's manager. Laughter prevailed upon Pike, who prevailed on the manager, and Glen came to the Bogey Busters to do the music. Because of his involvement with the Bogey Busters, Glen was introduced as a member at Bel-Air in the 1980s.

Glen was also friendly with a number of players on the PGA Tour, most notably Gay Brewer and Bobby Nichols. The Junior Chamber of Commerce in Los Angeles was having trouble raising the kinds of funds needed to maintain a competitive purse for the Los Angeles Open. At the time, a number of celebrities had their names attached to Tour events—Dean Martin, Joe Garagiola, Andy Williams, Bob Hope, Bing Crosby, Danny Thomas, and Sammy Davis Jr.

The L.A. Open was televised on CBS and it just so happened that Glen's show was on CBS as well. After some negotiation, the Glen Campbell Los Angeles Open was born and continued for a number of years.

Glen loved to play the game and, at one time, was a legitimate 3-handicap player. He was forever picking my brain for things that would help him make a better swing. I don't think I've ever been around him when we didn't talk about the golf swing or a piece of equipment. Most people don't know that he was an original investor in Lynx golf equipment, as was Andy Williams.

Golfers were a fraternity he liked, maybe even more than entertainment people. He loved to play in the Crosby. When he played, he played to win. As a musician, he succeeded because of work and love of the business. He had the same attitude about golf.

Pete Sampras

RELATIVELY NEW TO THE GAME, PETE SAMPRAS JOINED BEL-AIR in 2003 after retiring as perhaps the best tennis player in history. You can argue Tilden and Kramer; Laver, Newcombe, and Rosewall; Connors, Borg, and McEnroe. But if you take the measure of the best by the number of Grand Slam events won, the title goes far and away to Sampras.

Now he has a new love—other than his wife and children, of course—and that's golf. He's truly smitten. I've worked with him a time or two on his golf game, and I get the feeling that he's in this thing for the pure fun of it. Obviously, he has time, opportunity, and facilities to work on his game, but working at it is not something that appeals to him. He did that with tennis and it netted dividends. He doesn't intend to go through that rigor with golf.

He enjoys playing with his friends and he can hit a ball out of sight. He makes a lot of birdies, but he also hits a lot of shots that would make most of us turn our heads in fright. But that's the nature of the game and he understands that. That's the charm of golf that he finds appealing. He could be an accomplished player, if he truly set his mind to it. He's that great an athlete.

Pete reminds me a lot of Duffy Waldorf, the PGA Tour player who played for me at UCLA and whom I still teach. Duffy has immense talent, as does Pete. But both seem to place great value on dealing with family and friends and those people take priority in their lives. Everything else comes second.

I doubt we will see Pete competing in high-level amateur tournaments, although I suspect one day he could if he really wanted to. Instead, he's going to have fun and raise his family. Isn't that what we all should aspire to?

Spinout

WHEN YOU SPIN OUT OF A SHOT, YOU TURN your left hip to the left prematurely. Players who slice the ball ingrain that habit. I'm asking you to swing the handle over your left hip, but you can't do that if you've already spun your left hip out of the way. Put your feet close together, take  your left foot and drop it over your right foot, and hook your feet together. Now swing the handle with your forearms from one side of your body to the other.

With your feet locked, you cannot spin your hip to the left. You'll find it easier to draw the ball from this position. On the golf course, take your normal stance, concentrate on a belt loop that sits over your right hip. Take the club back, and when you swing to the left, keep that belt loop back as long as possible.

Star-Crossed

COREY PAVIN ALMOST LEFT UCLA IN HIS JUNIOR YEAR, WHICH at the time would have been a big blow to our program. He had been a first team All-American in his sophomore year, but the following year he didn't play well and was very despondent over the situation. When he didn't play well, he wasn't a happy camper.

He and his teacher friend, Bruce Hamilton, decided that maybe the best thing for him to do was turn pro. That decision, they believed, would solve all Corey's problems. I didn't agree because I didn't think Corey was as mature a young man as he might be, even though he was a heck of a player.

His family wanted him to finish school, so we had a get-together with his family and his teacher. My wife, Lisa, and my son Mason attended with me. It was on a Sunday afternoon at the Pavin home in Oxnard, and we had dinner and talked about this matter. It turned into quite a soul-searching affair where we all expressed ourselves with our hearts and minds. When it was all done, Corey decided to stay in school.

He decided to red-shirt the next year, which was his fourth year. He was behind in his credits and decided to take five years to finish four years' eligibility. Although he didn't play college golf that year, 1981, he did excel on the amateur level. He won the North and South Amateur at Pinehurst, won the Southwest Amateur in Arizona, played well in the Western

Amateur, qualified for the U.S. Open, and made the Walker Cup team. He also won the Maccabiah Games in Israel.

The next year, when he returned to the team, he was named college player of the year and led us to a number one ranking in college golf, the first time that had been achieved by a UCLA team. Pavin left quite a golfing legacy at UCLA. A portent of things to come for him.

One Drill, All Facets

STAND ERECT AND HOLD A CLUB AT THE HANDLE so that it extends straight in front of you. Now slide your hands up the shaft so they hold the club about halfway down the shaft. Move the club so that the grip end extends behind you past your left side.

With your elbows nice and free, move the club, with no backswing, to the left side of your body without the club hitting your side. That's the forward swing, which is the most important part. Golfers tend to be too backswing oriented. Both forearms combine to move the shaft to the left side of your body, which means over your left hip. Your hands don't manipulate the club—in fact, they never leave the starting position. They begin and remain at the side of the shaft and don't leave, never flipping over one another in the so-called release.

Now add the backswing. Swing the club over your right hip in the backswing. Swing the club to the left side of your body, over your left hip. Note that your body stays behind the shaft at all times during the swing. If your hands do manipulate the club in this drill, the top half of the shaft will wind up hitting your side at some point. If the shaft never hits you, the drill has been done properly. This drill teaches you everything you need to know about the golf swing.

Raymond Floyd

FLOYD WAS ONE OF THE GRITTIEST COMPETITORS I EVER KNEW. I had the opportunity in the early '70s to get to know him when he'd come to Bel-Air preparing for the winter tour. He would stay with the McCulloch family, who lived off the ninth tee at Bel-Air. He'd spend two or three weeks at Christmastime there, prepping for the Los Angeles Open.

During that time, he was in a bit of a slump, so I had occasion to work with him on the practice tee. I've always been impressed with Raymond in competition, especially when he's in the hunt. He gets that look in his eye that is unmistakable.

I'll never forget the 1986 U.S. Open at Shinnecock, with Jack Nicklaus, Greg Norman, Lee Trevino, and a number of others with a chance to win. You could see in Floyd's face the mask of concentration and determination when he headed into the final nine holes.

He didn't allow that mask of concentration to change until he'd reached the eighteenth green. He had a 2-stroke lead at that point and played his second shot onto the green, hit his approach putt some 2 feet below the hole, where he had a 2-putt to win, a 1-putt to win by 2. At that point, I can remember him marking the ball, then he looked up at his caddie, who was nicknamed Golf Ball, and winked. At this moment he came out of that concentration cocoon for the first time, but until then he was not about to let it get away. He didn't allow himself to celebrate too early.

Fairway Bunker

MOST GOLFERS ARE DEATHLY AFRAID OF THE fairway bunker shot. It can be made simple, provided you make a few preparations. As with all bunker shots, imagine the ball sitting on a tee and the tee completely covered with sand. The key to the fairway bunker shot is to get as much club on the ball as possible.

You do that with a couple of preparations. First, get your lower body stabilized, with equal weight on each leg. Then realize that you are going to hit the ball with your upper body only, primarily the forearms. With those preparations in mind, attempt to hit the ball at the equator or below. Don't hit on the upswing, because that will cause the club to hit the sand first. Don't hit down on the ball, because that drives the ball into the sand. Instead, attempt to be level with your swing and pick the ball off the sand. Stabilizing the weight and balance on both legs allows the clubhead to travel level with the sand surface for an extended period of time, making for better contact between club and ball.

Michael Bolton

A GREAT VOICE AND GOOD LOOKS DON'T NECESSARILY TRANSLATE into a good golf swing, but Michael Bolton is willing to learn. He's a fairly novice golfer, and I met him when he was a guest at Bel-Air. He was in Los Angeles for a film he was working on, and we had a few golf lessons during his downtime.

We talked about swing concept. Most golfers have swing habits and they have certain ideas, but they don't have a concept that is consistent. Michael was no different. He had no real understanding of what his swing should look and feel like.

If you think of any kind of athlete, it's pretty obvious what he does when he makes his delivery. Think of a sport and you can picture in your mind how the athlete makes a swing or throws a ball or propels it toward a target. But if you look down the line of players on a practice range, you will see forty different golf swings. They are all swinging based on the mental picture they have of the swing.

That's why golf is so difficult to learn. How can you expect to progress in the game if you don't have an image of the swing that allows you to have the confidence necessary to produce consistent shots? Michael was taught to swing from one side to the other. Each side of his swing had an end rather than a top. This allowed him to swing "through" rather than "to" the ball.

Horror Shots

THERE ARE FOUR HORROR SHOTS IN GOLF: THE top, the hook, the slice, and the shank.

The cold top is one that you quit on. As you near the ball in your swing, your forearms do not swing the handle through the ball, which means the handle is going backward. You quit on the shot. If you are lucky enough to hit the ball at all, it will go skittering along the ground.

The duck hook happens when your hands move from the side of the shaft. Your hands start on the side of the shaft at address, and when you swing the handle properly from one side of your body to the other, your hands never leave the sides of the shaft. But when you flip your hands over, your right hand is on top of the shaft and your left hand is under the shaft, causing a duck hook. By keeping your hands to the side of the shaft, you can't hook. Conversely, when your right hand is under the shaft and your left hand is on top, it's Slice City. It's the only way you can slice.

The shank, perish the thought, occurs when you swing the club open in the backswing and leave it open, with the heel of the club leading the toe into the ball. If you extend inside out, you bring the hosel—the part of the clubhead into which the shaft is fitted—into the ball. The cure: If you open the clubface on the backswing, you should extend your right arm to the left of the target when you strike the ball. In that way, you will work the heel of the club away from the ball instead of toward it. The best cure, however, involves timing—close the clubface in time.

Distance Line

WHEN YOU READ A PUTT, YOU HAVE THE DIREC- tion line in mind. It helps you get your bearings and it helps you relate to the hole and the line you want the ball to start on. But that's only half of it. You have to make the ball go the right distance as well.

Lay the flagstick directly behind the hole perpendicular to the target line. Cultivate the feeling of nursing the ball up to the second line that we call the "distance line." Like in pitching pennies, cultivate the feel of going the right distance. You do that by applying the right force to the ball with the handle of the putter.

Of course, you want to make the putt, but more than that, you want the ball to go the right distance. If you keep in mind the "distance line," you will have a lot more tap-ins for pars than 4-footers.

"The Dream Team"

MANY OF THE MORE MONUMENTAL OCCASIONS THAT OCCURRED AT Bel-Air were spawned at the infamous "Smart Table" (aptly dubbed by Carroll Shelby), where genius ebbed and flowed on a daily basis in direct proportion to the number of cocktails served.

One of these moments transpired in 1992 when a group of revelers decided a celebration was due to acknowledge my sixtieth birthday and thirty years of service to Bel-Air. It was conceived by members M. B. Scott, Bob Courtney, Mike Palmer, Joe Leach, Dick Crane, Bert Ladd, and Dick Traweek, all of whom were regulars at the Smart Table. It was decided to take me on a golfing odyssey to be remembered.

Thus was born the idea of "the Dream Team" junket to some of golf's greatest citadels in America: Pine Valley, Augusta National, and Seminole. Lots were drawn and the winning members were Jim Bowyer, Craig Crockwell, Richard Collis, Joe Leach, Bob Pecel, Larry Quilling, Ron Waranch, and Ed White to accompany me on a journey of memories.

Member Tony Novelly volunteered his beautiful Gulfstream II airplane complete with crew, foodstuffs, and plenty of liquid refreshments. The Dream Team express was off and flying on October 21 with first stop Philadelphia and transfer to the world's top-rated golf course, Pine Valley.

Two days and nights of housing in the famed Pine Valley dormlike "barracks" facilities with shared showers made for intriguing partnerships. The clubhouse menu was thoroughly exhausted by the Bel-Air boys in two days, and the bartender stated we had exceeded the previous two-day consumption record at Pine Valley (another Bel-Air first to be proud of back at the Smart Table). Great feats included Joe Leach's opening shot on the tenth hole, when he promptly put his ball into the famed "Devil's Anus." Collis won the two-day golf competition mainly because of his youth and stamina, a big advantage at Pine Valley. His birdie at the eighteenth eked out an overtime win over Bob Pecel. Pecel received the "shot-of-the-trip" award when his explosion shot from the front bunker at the fourteenth stuck on the face of his wedge as he finished the stroke. Not knowing what to do at this point, Bob decided to appeal his case beyond the not-so-friendly confines of his golfing opponents to the highest courts, the USGA and the R&A. His ongoing saga was recorded for history.

Ernest Ransome, the legendary chairman at Pine Valley, entertained us in his home for cocktails on our first night, where he introduced us to our playing hosts, one of whom was Club President Mel Dickenson. We dined that evening at Ernie's favorite Italian restaurant in Clementon, detouring before bed to one of Jersey's infamous truck stops for a "final final" in memory of the guys who didn't come on the trip.

The truckers did not take too nicely to the "boys from Bel-Air." Perhaps our natty attire miscast us. Heeding the sage advice of Bowyer and Quilling, we copped a plea of sanity and beat a hasty retreat to the comfortable confines of our dormitory while we were still intact.

Day three dawned and we sadly bid farewell to Pine Valley in all its greatness accented in the Indian summer colors of late October. After a hearty breakfast, our caravan offed to the Philadelphia airport, thirty miles away, where our "Novelly express" was readied. Along the way, Pecel continued his appeal regarding the "stuck-on-the-clubface" ruling. It was a good case but to no avail.

On to Augusta! The odyssey continued with the ongoing gin rummy tournament commencing as soon as the Dream Team were aboard the Gulfstream. If golf was the passion, gin rummy was the forte for this squad. Who would be the victor? This would not be determined until we landed in New Orleans at the end of the trip. White and Crockwell were early favorites. Let the battle continue!

A no-smoking rule prevailed during the Pine Valley segment of the trip but was set free as soon as we left New Jersey. This was a welcome sign at Augusta National, because chairman Jack Stephens, who was there to greet us, was an avowed smoker, as was Bobby Jones before him. The Dream Team was made to feel at home! Host members Bob Berry, Frank Broyles, and Rex Cross, in their green jackets, were our guides for two days of golfing heaven. It does not get any better than Augusta National.

The famed Butler Cabin was made our home away from

home for the two days. We even had our own private green jacket presentation that put the Masters Ceremony to shame. If only Cliff Roberts knew, we might never get back into the state of Georgia.

Golf was keen, with thirty-six holes plus a special round on the par-3 course featured in the competition. Joe Leach and Larry Quilling were supreme in their play. Bob Pecel's 6-iron shot at the twelfth hung on the lip of the hole for an ace! He is still moaning. He was one inch away from $1,000 anted up by the team.

Predinner cocktails were served in the Butler Cabin with our green-jacketed Augusta hosts in attendance. We were joined in residence by the National's two golf pros, Bob Klepke and Dave Spencer. Dinner in the clubhouse is a rare experience. Each table is occupied by green-jacketed members and their guests, who dine in regal surroundings under the watchful eyes cast in the hanging portraits of Dwight Eisenhower, Bobby Jones, and Clifford Roberts. Their influence is overpowering! The Southern-style dinner was complemented by wines from one of this country's best cellars. The Dream Team did enjoy themselves.

Taking our leave from Augusta was not easy. It is, as Jack Nicholson says, "as good as it gets." But Seminole was awaiting on day six and our wheels were up at 9:00 A.M., and off to Florida we went.

From the Palm Beach airport we were whisked to the Seminole Golf Club, where we were welcomed by members Denny Phipps, Mickey Van Gerbig, and brother Barry Van Gerbig, the club president. They hosted their Bel-Air guests at a lovely luncheon just off the locker room, which is considered the finest in America.

Golf that afternoon was a treat on one of Donald Ross's great courses, which was sculptured over the Florida dunes in the 1920s at the behest of Seminole founding member E. F. Hutton. Joe Leach and Ed White set the pace, with Ron Waranch and Mickey Van Gerbig leaving the course early to see the sights on Worth Avenue. Larry Quilling, responding to a pregame lesson from the Little Pro, was the day's big winner, with Collis second.

Our hotel, the Brazilian Court, was a famous stopping place for the Kennedy clan. The Palm Beach nightspots were nothing the Dream Team couldn't handle with aplomb. Conversation ebbed and flowed about Seminole's wind, Bermuda grass, and 192 bunkers.

Bel-Air member Ken Slutsky arranged a bonus round at Old Marsh, where he was part owner. Greg Norman made this his home club until he built the Medalist Club. Young Rob McNamara, a candidate for Bel-Air's new assistant pro job from Kentucky, joined us for golf and recorded a 67 on the round. Play on this day was highlighted by the now infamous "Palmetto Bush" shot.

Ron Waranch's ball at the tenth hole became ensconced at the base of one of Florida's indigenous rapier-leaved palmettos. His options were to take an unplayable lie 1-stroke penalty or try to forge through a small opening straight ahead and suffer the consequences. Partner Jim Bowyer, because of the enormity of their wagers, tried all his powers of persuasion to convince his partner that the wiser choice was to take the penalty and avoid the risks. Disregarding the brotherly advice, Waranch reasoned that his success in life had been due to taking a few calculated risks. So he plowed straight ahead.

The perils of the palmetto proved to be too much even for the talented Waranch. His play was halted for medical and mental attention. To the chagrin of the other bettors, the game had to come to an abrupt end with one of our warriors impaled by his own decision.

Off to New Orleans at four o'clock in the afternoon on our seventh day, a fitting final chapter to our legendary journey. This town is where I received my graduate training before my professional career took me to Merion, Thunderbird, Rockaway Hunt, Westchester, and then to Bel-Air. It would be fitting to see the old haunts.

The Windsor Court Hotel was our home for the last two nights. We encountered Bel-Air member Chris Hemmeter there at his residence while he pursued his ill-fated efforts to secure the hotel gambling rights on the riverfront. Dinner that evening was enjoyed at the famed Antoine's restaurant across Bourbon Street from my favorite stopping place, the Absinth House Bar.

A special treat was arranged for the Dream Team on Saturday morning, which happened to be Halloween day. The New Orleans Country Club, which had been my adopted club during my school days at LSU, hosted our entire team in a friendly final match on our tour of tours. Four former club presidents served as our golfing hosts, then entertained us at a luncheon featuring Louisiana red beans and rice. New Orleans Country Club pro Gordon Johnson filled in for the ailing Ron Waranch.

R & R in the afternoon prepared us for our final evening, which was a fitting climax to a great trip. The Dream Team in the French Quarter on Halloween night. It does get better, after all, Jack!

Awards were declared at the final dinner, with Richard Collis nosing out Quilling, Leach, and Bowyer for the golfing award, and Craig Crockwell edging Ed White for the gin rummy title. A panel of impartial impersonators declared Jim Bowyer the "best-looking Dream Teamer" in a too-close-to-call contest against Leach, Waranch, and Collis. Ed White was "most improved player," and Bob Pecel was "hard-luck player of the trip."

Back to the reality world of Bel-Air after nine days in a golfer's fantasy world. It makes us realize we don't have it too bad here after all.

Amy Alcott

AS A YOUNG GIRL, AMY ALCOTT WAS AS FINE A TALENT AS YOU could find. What she needed was a mentor, someone wise in the ways of the world who could oversee her progress in the game, to teach her what she would need on the course to become a champion.

Fortunately, Amy had that mentor in the person of Walter Keller, who was the first golf professional to open a retail off-course golf store. He did so over the objections of his fellow green-grass professionals but today is considered a forerunner in the way golf equipment is sold to the public.

He was a member of Riviera Country Club in Los Angeles, and there he became acquainted with young Amy. He volunteered to help her with her competitive golf game. Not only did he help her with the technical aspects of the game, he also helped her gain entry into junior and women's amateur tournaments.

So good was Amy that she won the U.S. Girls Junior at age seventeen and she decided to skip college and head directly into the ranks of the LPGA Tour. As an eighteen-year-old rookie, she won her first tournament and thus started a career that ended with her induction into the LPGA Hall of Fame.

That journey almost didn't have a happy ending. The LPGA hall is the toughest to get into in all of sport. At the time, you needed thirty victories in LPGA-sanctioned tournaments, and Amy was stuck, from age thirty-four, at twenty-nine wins. She also had five majors, but majors didn't count any more than regular tour wins.

Then, thank goodness, the LPGA changed its entrance requirements and began to give extra weight to major championships, and Amy was duly inducted into her deserving place in the Hall of Fame.

Along the way, the members at Bel-Air made her an honorary member of the club and, as such, she pays back that honor by playing regularly with our members. She is seen here quite often, practicing and lending her experience and expertise to the members.

She came to me in the early 1990s, after what most would consider a good season. But she was having trouble with her putting. I had just assumed that she was and always had been a good putter, but I had come to find out otherwise.

So we worked on her putting and she liked the things we worked on. What I tried to do was give her a system that covered all the learning she needed. As she played and practiced, day by day, she could become more confident. She had a chance to win the 1994 U.S. Women's Open, finishing tied for sixth.

She came back to Bel-Air sometime later, having a devil of a time hooking the ball. She was also blocking the ball to the right, the flip side of the same problem. We went down to the practice tee and within a matter of about fifteen minutes, we solved her problem in a pretty simple way. It was important that we not interfere with her swing style. The last thing I wanted was to blow her mind with swing theory and conflicting ideas that might disrupt her confidence.

But she pressed on. She started asking questions about other things, and I could sense that this could be a problem. With Amy, one question leads to another, and whatever we were working on in the beginning becomes totally obscured. She began searching her own technique for answers that actually disrupted her confidence.

From the time she was eighteen, through twenty-nine LPGA Tour victories, she never doubted what she was doing. She played with the swing she developed under Walter Keller, an effective style that would produce and reproduce time and again. She always knew what the effect was going to be. She played well by instinct and repetition, but when she asks too many questions, problems surface and confidence wanes and real problems develop.

What I admire about Amy is that she is a great proponent of women's golf and she has been a great example of what the game can produce. She is wonderful with people, and I see that especially when she interacts with the Bel-Air members. Some touring professionals don't have the personality to do well in that arena, but Amy really does.

Roll the Ball

AMY WAS WHAT I CONSIDER A POP PUTTER. SHE used to pop the head of the putter at the ball. She "hit" the ball rather than "rolling" the ball, which I prefer. That comes from a controlled stroke where you accent the handle of the putter as opposed to the head of the putter in trying to move it through the ball.

So I was trying to draw her attention away from the putter head and focus it on the other end of the putter. I wanted to have her make her stroke there and develop a feeling of rolling the ball rather than popping or hitting the ball. Once you get the ball rolling, it is just a matter of distance and direction, which she could account for easily enough because she could read greens well and had a good enough feel for distance.

Mikhail Baryshnikov

I HAVE A REMINDER IN THE FORM OF A PLAQUE IN MY DEN OF THE day I gave Mikhail Baryshnikov a golf lesson. That was also the day my wife, Lisa, had her first hole in one on the par-3 tenth hole at Bel-Air. All kinds of pandemonium broke out after the shot. James Garner was playing right behind Lisa's group, and James Woods, Mac Davis, and the Japanese baseball great Sadaharu Oh were all on hand for that momentous occasion. In fact, they all signed Lisa's card and it's now on our wall.

Baryshnikov was on hand for all the buzz, and for a person who is accustomed to dealing with applause and adoration, he had probably never seen such excitement over a golf shot. He was in Los Angeles for a performance he was to give in Santa Barbara the next night. And, as unpretentious as he is, he recognized Lisa before the performance for her hole in one and made her feel as if she were the star of the show.

Baryshnikov is an avid golfer and belongs to a club near Jacksonville, Florida, where he has a home. He has great balance and posture, which you would expect from someone as gifted and athletic as he is. He also has great strength.

But, like most other golf players, he complains of a lack of distance.

In treating that malady, we didn't address the strength factors as much as we looked at grip, setup, and positioning. He had his left hand too much on top of the grip. When you do that, you immobilize the use of your left arm. With such a grip, you are likely to overuse your hands at the expense of the strength of your body. I prefer to see the hands set more to the side of the club. When you have your hands in a neutral position, they have a passive role in the swing and therefore you can use the strength of your body.

Grip changes can be painful, and it was no different with Baryshnikov. But he understood that changes in the golf swing can be like changes in a ballet routine. You have to practice a lot.

Most players set the club on the ground and then fit their hands to the club. If you set your hands on the club in a grounded position, it becomes very difficult to change or make small adjustments. First of all, you can't feel the club. You are trying to liven the grip with a dead club. I prefer that you hold the club in the air when you address it. Then not only can you feel it, but you also can make adjustments in midair. You are made to see that the fit of your hands are to the side of the grip as opposed to on top or underneath. It's similar to gripping a tennis racket. You grip to the side in line with the face of the racket. You do that when the racket is in the air. You don't grip the racket while it's lying on the ground.

One-Arm Swing

SWING YOUR CLUB WITH ONE ARM ONLY. HOLD the handle of the club in your right hand and use your right forearm to turn the club to the right. Notice that the turn came from your right forearm. That turned the club, your shoulder, and your hip to the right. Notice that the upper part of your  arm has lifted up and your hand hinged at the wrist.

Let's reverse. Your right arm caused the turn in the backswing and in the downswing it unfolded, causing much of the power and all the direction of the shot. Your arm has extended through the shot. Try to hit a ball with your right arm only. It's a great strength-training drill.

As you swing away from the ball in the backswing, your left arm is going to give you extension. When you reverse, the lower muscle in your forearm is gradually covering the ball, causing the turn of the club through the ball to the left. There's no release or flipping over of the hand. You are gradually moving the club to the left side of your body. With your elbow free, you use your forearm to move the club to the finish. That causes a turn of the club, your shoulder, and your hip to the left. This drill explains the role of each arm (active) and both hands (passive), and helps you to locate and understand your swing plane.

Setting the Right Side

THERE ARE CERTAIN POINTS IN THE RIGHT SIDE to be set correctly. At address, set your right wrist inward, your right knee inward, and your right elbow inward. Now you're all set and ready to go and move forward through the shot. Make a backswing and try to retain that inward set.  Keep your right wrist inward and away from laying the club off or out of plane. Keep your right elbow inward and prevent it from flying away. And keep your right knee inward and not buckled to the outside. The net result is that at all times you are set to move forward. If you get out of position, you have to recover and move back into position.

John Williams

WITHIN ITS MEMBERSHIP, BEL-AIR COULD FIELD QUITE A CHORAL group of its own, including Glen Campbell, Bing Crosby, Mac Davis, Howard Keel, Bob Goulet, John Raitt, Glen Frey, Dean Martin, Hoagy Carmichael, Andy Williams, Jo Stafford, Engelbert Humperdinck, and Dorothy Kirsten. Accompany these with the orchestrations of Les Brown, Paul Weston, Tutti Camaratta, Lawrence Welk, and Sonny Burke, and you have music for the ages.

Who, though, would be best qualified to lead this group? None other than John T. Williams of Academy Award and Boston Pops fame. The maestro of our times.

As a golfer, John T. plays to cap his day, which has been spent composing and directing. He enjoys nothing more than a casual nine-hole round at four o'clock in the afternoon. I have had the privilege of accompanying him on many of these lighthearted treks that are so meaningful to him.

On one of these afternoon walks in late December, I broached the subject of the upcoming Rose Parade in which he was to serve as the grand marshall, a title reserved for the most eminent. Curious, I asked him which side he would sit on during the football game that culminated the Rose Parade festivities. Would it be USC or would it be Michigan? His answer was classic John T. Williams: "After the coin toss I think I will politely excuse myself and go back to Bel-Air for nine holes," which he did do. His work was done and he needed his late-afternoon ritual. A true golfer, indeed!

Complementing the 1999 Ryder Cup matches at the Country Club in Brookline, Williams conducted two concerts with the Boston Pops celebrating the occasion. The first honored the two teams, with Celine Dion serenading the audience to the delight of Captains Ben Crenshaw and Mark James, the teams, and their followers. The second was a tribute to Arnold Palmer, the American icon, with president-to-be George W. Bush in attendance.

No one has more reverence for the game and those who play it than the stylish nine-holer John Williams. Rhythm is his forte!

The Championship Year

IN 1988, WE HAD FOUR PLAYERS COME BACK WHO HAD COMPETED in the NCAA Championships the previous year. We also had four different players win tournaments that year, but all in all, it wasn't a good year for UCLA golf.

In the Pac-10 Conference championship, we finished eighth of ten teams. In those days, a committee within your district had the discretion to vote teams into the NCAA Championships based on the year's performance. By all rights, we should not have been voted in, but we were, I suspect on the basis of past performance. It was an absolute gift that we were in the field.

The tournament was played at North Ranch, north of Los Angeles, and hosted by Southern Cal, the first time the Trojans had ever hosted a national championship in golf. We played the Southwest Intercollegiate at North Ranch for a few years, and the last hole had been a virtual graveyard for us. One year, we came into the final hole with a 9-shot lead and lost 12 shots on the last hole.

So we didn't have a very good feeling about the course. The NCAA set up the course with high Bermuda rough, and the fairways there are serpentine, bendy landing areas. We had a team of long hitters, and with the tight fairways and high rough, I thought we were hamstrung from the start. Our team of Brandt Jobe, Bob Lasken, Kevin Leach, Richard Greenwood, and Tim Cruickshank thought otherwise.

As it turned out, with the tight course, coaches were taking drivers out of the hands of their players and most were driving with 1- or 2-irons, and all of a sudden we're the longest driving team because our guys can hit their long irons farther than most. At that point, things started to look up for us. We had four tournament winners on our team, and only two other teams in the field—Oklahoma State and Arizona— could say that.

Those two teams were favored and no one was paying much attention to us. When the final round began we were in fifth place, 13 strokes behind Florida. We were paired with Oklahoma and Georgia Tech. At the sixteenth hole, Oklahoma was leading the tournament, until Glen Day 4-putted from 15 feet and there was a 3-shot swing.

We got to the graveyard hole, and I remember walking from the seventeenth green to the eighteenth tee—I had experienced too much angst at that hole in previous tournaments. I encountered Brandt Jobe, and I told him that I didn't care what club he took off the tee, just to "swing it as positively as you can."

He flat-nailed the tee shot and only had a 9-iron into the green. All of our five players made par on that hole. Florida, Southern Cal, and Oklahoma all collapsed down the stretch, and when the dust settled, we were the champions. We never led the tournament until the last hole.

It was the strangest feeling that ever overcame me. There was joy and elation, but I also had this feeling of absolute calm. In the interview afterward, I used a word I'd never used before: *dumbfounded*. I really was dumbfounded. The golf gods decided it was time for us to win a national championship.

That was my thirteenth year with the program, and it was the culmination of a lot of sweat and effort and determination. Originally we thought that when we took over in 1975, we could win the nationals in five years. We were a little behind schedule, but it was no less satisfying. It wasn't a team of superstars. We didn't have a Corey Pavin or a Duffy Waldorf or a Tom Pernice. But they were a wonderful group of young men. It was no doubt the crowning achievement of their golf careers.

Jack Nicholson

I'VE SEEN A NUMBER OF CELEBRITIES LEARN THE GAME OF GOLF and find a whole new life. Jack Nicholson is one of the prime examples. Golf lets him use all his energy, and he has found much fascination in learning the basics and the nuances of the game, trying all the while to get better.

However, he's not one to count each and every stroke he takes. He might take a second serve on occasion. But when he is forced to put pencil to scorecard, he can still play pretty well, as evidenced by the fact that he won one of our member-guest tournaments at Bel-Air. When his photograph was taken holding the little trophy for winning, he had that patented Nicholson smile from ear to ear.

I have a photo taken at a clinic I was giving at nearby Sherwood Country Club, where Nicholson and Joe Pesci are also members. I was holding a practice club, and in the foreground of the picture, Nicholson and Pesci are looking at me with rapt attention.

Funny, it's usually the other way around.

Shoulder Rotation

THE SHOULDERS AREN'T REALLY MADE TO TILT.
If the shoulders tilt, it's actually a spine tilt. The shoulders are made to rotate. Grab your arms at the elbows, with your elbows in the palms of your hands as if you were cradling a baby. Swing your torso to the right and keep your elbows  level. If your elbows go up and down, you'll lose that precious cargo. Swing your elbows to the right and then to the left. In that way, your shoulders, your hips, and your knees are all working on the same level, which is ideal. More than that, your arms are moving from right to left in sync with the torso.

Joe Pesci

HE WAS THE POET LAUREATE OF BEL-AIR, AND WHILE HIS LAN-guage might not be exquisite, it's certainly colorful. That, I suppose, is due to his background of trying to make a living in New York as an actor, tending bar and whatever else one has to do to survive such an existence.

He learned to play golf there, among a group that liked to gamble quite a bit. His street smarts served him well, and he developed some know-how for learning to play well within his handicap limits.

He's not a big man, but he has a good medium-sized swing even though he looks like a whirling dervish through the ball. His body and his club are forever tying to catch up with one another.

We were partners in the Michael Douglas and Friends tournament in Las Vegas. Our team was Kenny G, Martin Sheen, Matthew McConaughey, Pesci, and me. We won on the strength of Kenny G and Pesci. He feels comfortable in front of the camera, and when the red light goes on, he knows how to perform.

On winning, we all got a hug and a kiss from Catherine Zeta-Jones. Not bad!

Simple Math

PLAYING IN THE WIND OR TO ELEVATION changes is a matter of simple math. For every mile an hour the wind blows, the playing distance changes by a yard. For instance, if the wind is blowing 20 mph in your face, the shot plays as if it's twenty yards longer than the actual distance. The  opposite is true downwind. A 10-mph helping wind will make the shot play ten yards shorter.

The same holds true for elevation changes. For every foot of elevation change, the net effect is one yard of change. If the green is ten feet above the level on which you are standing, the shot plays ten yards longer. The opposite is true for downhill shots. Your mental computer needs to compute these variables in order to arrive at effective distance.

The Bubsy

A LOT OF AWARDS HAVE COME MY WAY THROUGH THE YEARS, ALL of which I am very grateful for. None is more pleasing than the Man of the Year tribute at "the Bubsy" golf outing in Reno in 1997.

The occasion involves some three hundred men gathering

in the desert to raise money in support of the Richstone Foundation, which cares for battered and abandoned children. Golf and fun and games are the highlights.

The event was conceived and directed by Richard P. Crane, Bob Courtney, and Dick Traweek. Crane, one of Bel-Air's great presidents, had an abiding love for the endeavor, which honored his own son who was tragically lost in a mountain hiking accident. Courtney, whose wife headed the Richstone Foundation, is the Bubsy's heart and soul. A champion of the little man, it is his nickname, Bubsy, that carries the banner. Traweek, who brokered the sale of Pebble Beach, is the Perle Mesta of golf tournaments, an organizer without peer.

These gentlemen have been great friends of the Little Pro and I am proud of the association.

Club Choice

IF YOU ARE IN A QUANDARY AS TO WHICH CLUB to use for a particular shot, remember to have enough club to reach the back edge of the green so you can swing comfortably to get the ball to the target. If you are still debating between clubs, go with the club you are the most confident in. And chase  any negative thoughts you have down the avenue. Choose the club and be positive.

Scott McCarron

PLAYING COLLEGE GOLF IN THE MODERN ERA, JUST LIKE OTHER college athletics, isn't an easy proposition. Being a student takes a considerable amount of time. And golf, by its very nature, is time-consuming. So, if you're going to be a top-caliber college golfer, you need to watch your time carefully.

At least that was my philosophy as the UCLA golf coach. But with Scott McCarron, who's to say I was right? Scott came along when Duffy Waldorf and Steve Pate were still in school. And he chose to pledge a fraternity when he hit campus. I didn't think that was such a good idea, that he might have spread himself too thin with school, golf, and fraternity life.

I suppose he enjoyed his five years in college, but I don't think he fulfilled his promise as a player. He came to UCLA as the Northern California Junior champion. As it happened, we won the NCAA Championship in 1988, his last year in school. But he didn't make the five-man team that went to the tournament.

After he left school, he struggled a bit for a couple of years and even thought about joining his father in the clothing business and giving up his dream of becoming a professional player. But he discovered a solution to his old nemesis, putting, with a homemade long putter, and shortly thereafter he qualified for the PGA Tour.

Since then, he has been an unqualified success. He is

enjoying a wonderful career, and when he putts well, he's a match for anyone.

So who knows? Maybe pledging a fraternity is the way to go, after all.

Three States of the Cat

THE FIRST STATE OF THE CAT: LYING IN THE corner sound asleep, totally relaxed and totally out of it. The second state: ready to leap in the athletic position. Mentally, he's relaxed and all his joints are free. The third state: perish the thought, stiff as a board lying in the street. This is a state in which anxious players find themselves with every joint totally locked. The joints should be perfectly free, but the muscle system is in use. Be the second state of the cat before you swing and during your swing. The muscles are in use like rubber bands, but the joints must be free in order to transmit the swing.

Living Large

KERRY PACKER, THE AUSTRALIAN BILLIONAIRE MEDIA MAGNATE, is truly a larger-than-life character. He is the wealthiest man in Australia and one of the richest in the world. I first met him in 1978 when we visited Australia thanks to the People to People exchange program. We met through a mutual friend, Jack McCarthy, a member at the Australian Golf Club, who used to bring Packer along on his trips to the United States. They loved to stop by Bel-Air on the way to Pebble Beach and swap stories, as well as book lessons with me.

He's a large man in physical size and even larger in stature. The word *no* is not in the Packer vocabulary. Once, when he couldn't buy television rights to the Test cricket matches in Australia, he formed his own teams of cricket superstars to compete on his Channel Nine television station.

He often stopped by Bel-Air on his way to Las Vegas, where he liked to test his wits against the casino owners, who lived in fear of the way Packer gambled, which is to say in the millions. He liked to consider himself a backgammon expert, and he loved other forms of gambling. He had a habit of hitting casinos for upward of $10 million at a time, which would ruin the hotel's bottom line for the next quarter. But he also left that kind of money on the table on other occasions and became known as the number one casino gambler in the world.

In 1980, my UCLA golf team was to play in the NCAA Championships on the Scarlet Course at Ohio State. We arrived on Sunday, the day before practice rounds began. It so happened that Sunday was the final round of the Memorial Tournament at Jack Nicklaus's Muirfield Village. Packer was on hand—he has a cottage next to Jack's on the property—and he invited the entire team and coaches to Muirfield to watch the final round of the Memorial as his guests.

They were treated like absolute royalty, and it became a memory those young men would long treasure. As we prepared for the NCAA Championship that week, Packer, McCarthy, and the rest of the "Australian Mafia," as they were fondly known, came to cheer us on. We finished way down the line, but not for lack of support.

Into the 1980s, Packer would come by Bel-Air on his way to the AT&T Pebble Beach Pro-Am, where he was the partner of Greg Norman. He'd stop off for golf lessons to prepare for Pebble. One year, we arranged for my son Mason to caddie for Packer in the AT&T. It was an experience the likes of which he could only imagine.

He was whisked off to Monterey in Packer's airplane, which had flown in many of the Australian players who were to compete at Pebble. Mason was given an automobile to drive while in Monterey, he was housed by Packer, and he played practice rounds in the company of Nicklaus, Tom Watson, and other great players.

McCarthy told me before the tournament, "Mason is a lad of twenty-four embarking on this journey with Packer. When he returns in a week, he will be a ripe old man of forty."

In the early '90s, Packer came through Bel-Air on his way to the AT&T and was recovering from an accident in Australia, when he suffered a heart attack and fell off a polo pony during a match. He was technically dead for the better part of a minute and was resuscitated by equipment on hand for the occasion.

After recovering, he asked the prime minister how many of those resuscitation units were available. On learning that only half the sites recommended had the necessary equipment, he told the prime minister that he would provide the equipment at his expense.

Because of the illness, his handicap for the AT&T had been increased from 10 to 19. By the time he arrived at Pebble Beach, he was back to the top of his health, but his handicap stayed the same, much to the consternation of the other competitors, who thought he should have half the allotted strokes. As a result, Packer and Norman won the pro-am portion of the tournament that year, one of Packer's many crowning achievements.

I enjoyed working with Packer as a student because when he came for a lesson, he was there to get better, not just to spend the time of day for a fee. He was a good test for a teacher because he questioned whatever you had to say. As one of the richest men in the world, he is not without opinions. Nor was I the only teacher he had ever sought advice from. So you had better be on your toes with Packer, and whatever you had to say to him had to make sense and be something he could put into immediate practice.

Still, it was fun to engage in a battle of wills with Packer, and I always look forward to his return.

Once, when we were visiting Muirfield Village, we were staying in the Packer cottage. He thought there should be a Jacuzzi and called the people whose business was to sell and install such things. He was told that he could have a Jacuzzi in seven days. Packer told the man on the other end of the phone that he hadn't understood the question, that a Jacuzzi needed to be installed in two days, and for a certain price, he expected this to be done. It was.

Like I said, *no* is not in Kerry Packer's vocabulary.

The late Jack Grout, Nicklaus's longtime teacher, could have testified to that fact. On one visit, Packer arranged for a playing lesson from Grout that was to take the better part of a day. I was within the Nicklaus clubhouse, and other family members were staring intently out the window down the eighteenth fairway, wondering where Packer and Grout could be.

Presently, they came riding down the middle of the fairway about 8:00 P.M., caddie hanging off the back of the golf cart, violating all of Nicklaus's rules about carts remaining on the paths. Packer hit three shots from the middle of the fairway onto the green and putted out, much to the relief of Grout.

But Pack was not done. He ordered the caddie to dump out a bag of practice balls behind the bunker beside the eighteenth green, whereby he hit pitch and bunker shots until dark.

Unfortunately, Grout died some months later. I'm certain he always remembered the day Packer rode him like a race-horse.

Coordination

SOMEWHERE IN THE SCHEME OF THINGS, YOUR legs have a role to play. Your legs are in a support role, reacting to what your arms are doing. But you need to include the use of the legs. Let's do that with a drill, which I call the baseball drill. You are going to coordinate rhythm, tempo, contact, and timing with this drill.

Address the ball and draw your forward leg back even with the back leg. Now you are in a baseball stance with your feet together in the back of the batter's box. You are going to make a stride forward to hit the ball, and to do this you have to station more weight on your right leg to start with. If you are on your left leg, you can't move into the ball. Now, as you stride forward, you are going to go ahead and hit the shot.

Your legs provide the lateral thrust that adds up to 20 percent of the total distance of the shot. When you move into the ball, your left leg feels as if it's pulling your body, and at the same time your right leg pushes, which gives you a lateral thrust. It would be like standing with your feet tied together and trying to throw a ball. You could throw it only so far. But if you use your legs to get a running start, you throw it that much farther.

It's good practice to add this step in your practice swing. The step forward with your left leg is simultaneous with the movement of the handle of the club to the right. In effect, you are creating a scissors effect with your body: Your upper body is moving to the right, but your lower body is beginning to move to the left. That scissors effect is creating an elasticity in your body, allowing you to spring through the ball.

The Announcers

GOLF HAS BEEN BLESSED WITH GREAT BROADCASTERS WHO EMBELlish what we see on television with their candid tones. At Bel-Air I have had the privilege of knowing the very best in their business.

Keith Jackson, "Mr. College Football," has been a 2-handicap golfer at both Bel-Air and Los Angeles Country Club. He covered the U.S. Amateur at Bel-Air for ABC in 1976, an event won by Bill Sander of Seattle over C. Parker Moore of South Carolina.

Al Michaels, considered the best all-around commentator on ABC Sports, currently has the distinction of playing more golf at Bel-Air than any other member. His coverage of golf's Shoot Out Under the Lights at Sherwood, Big Horn, and The Bridges at Rancho Santa Fe lends to his versatility. He previously anchored the Skins Game. Al is soon on the scene the next day for golf after *Monday Night Football*.

Jim Nantz is now doing football and basketball as well as golf for CBS. Who knows, now that the president of sports is in charge of news at CBS, maybe Jim will become the next Walter Cronkite! Golf remains his passion, however, beginning with his college days with Fred Couples and company at the University of Houston. He is a good player who knows the nuances of the game. Better yet, he gives unsparingly of his time and talent.

Vince Scully is without challenge as a baseball announcer. He is synonymous with the Dodgers. Venturing into golf coverage presented new challenges for the neophyte golfer Scully. I remember him booking time with me to discuss golf history, language, and traditions before he anchored the CBS Masters coverage in the 1980s. As in baseball, he never went into the broadcast booth unprepared. Vince went on to cover the Skins Game and the Grand Slam of Golf. He worked later for NBC with sidekicks Bruce Devlin and Lee Trevino. Vinnie, as he is affectionately known, likes nothing more than a casual stroll around Bel-Air with Christopher Lee, Dan Cathcart, John Pike, or Ed White, discussing Shakespeare, current events, or world affairs. The golf, though serious, is purely recreational.

Jack Whitaker, the poet laureate of golf and the master wordsmith, emcees our Friends of Golf day and evening each year. His love for the game manifests in the fact that he is a member of Shinnecock and Merion, two of golf's great traditions. A longtime regular on both CBS and ABC, Jack hosted the Shell Wonderful World of Golf for both Terry Jastrow and Frank Chirkinian. His respect and devotion make the game of golf a better place.

The Sultan of Johor

GOLF ATTRACTS ALL SORTS OF DIGNITARIES, FROM PRESIDENTS TO senators to star athletes to star celebrities. But rarely does one come across a sultan, as I did in the early 1990s.

The sultan of Johor, a province in Malaysia, was in Los Angeles, where he was having his G4 aircraft custom fitted. He was also being custom fitted for golf clubs at Callaway Golf Company in Carlsbad, about ninety minutes down Interstate 5.

Having brand-new golf equipment and no place to play, the Callaway people suggested he pay a visit to Bel-Air. So appreciative was the sultan of our hospitality, he invited Lisa and me to visit him in Johor.

The trip came straight out of a fairy tale. It's difficult to describe in vivid enough detail the splendor that unfolded before our eyes. He has his own polo grounds and stables that house some two hundred polo ponies. His garage holds seventy-five automobiles. He has a hangar on the palace grounds for his helicopter. His G4 aircraft stands at the ready at the nearby Johor Airport so that he can go anywhere he chooses at a moment's notice. He has his own zoo and ocean-going yacht.

He has never stopped at traffic lights, either flying over them in his helicopter or running through them as his motorcade takes over the streets, led by motorcycle escort. That's the way he went to the golf course every day he played. We'd take the helicopter and land adjacent to the clubhouse, and we were escorted to the first tee, where three caddies awaited. One caddie went ahead to shoo away the other golfers. We played through everyone on the course. Another caddie teed up the sultan's ball and held his cigarette. The third caddie pictured the shot for him and gave him his club.

Since this was his country, he made the rules. If he wanted to concede a 10-foot putt—his or yours—he did so. But if he wanted you to putt from 6 inches, you obeyed without question.

The sultan was a mechanic at heart. He loved getting a new airplane or car and sitting up half the night reading the manuals—not about how to drive or fly, but how to build it. While we were there, a Callaway club arrived in the middle of a luncheon. It was delivered to the sultan's table, whereby he asked for a swingweight scale. He unwrapped the club and weighed it, making certain that it was made precisely to the specs he ordered.

Lisa spent much of her time with the sultan's wife. It's not a custom to have a drink of alcohol in Johor, but Lisa didn't let that stop her. Lisa, the sultan's wife, and the sultan's sister found a way to come up with a cocktail of choice, whether the sultan liked it or not.

I guess we know who really rules Johor.

Rhythm

RHYTHM IS DIFFERENT FROM TEMPO OR TIM-
ing, in that rhythm deals with putting the
optimum speed at the right place in the
swing. Tempo deals with the rate of speed
in the swing. And the timing of the swing
from one side of the body to the other determines the curve of the shot.

With rhythm, in every swing, you create an optimum
speed. It does you no good if the top speed occurs at the end
of the backswing, midway down to the ball, or at the finish.
The optimum speed should be at the ball.

That means away from the ball as well as through the ball.
You can swing the club away from the ball as fast as you are
comfortable with, but you have to come set at the end of the
backswing. By the same token, your speed must be optimal
through the ball, but you slow down to finish on balance.

Address the ball and get set to play the shot. When you
swing the club away from the ball, do it as fast as you feel
comfortable with. But when you do, say a little cadence.
When you get to the end of your backswing, say "Set." And
when you start forward, say "Swing."

If you like a drill, try this: Stand in the middle of a doorway and swing a club, off the ground, between the sides of
the doorway. One side of the doorway represents the end of
the backswing and the other side represents the end of the
forward swing. Say "Set" on one side of the doorway and

"Swing" in the middle. It will improve your sense of rhythm and, in the bargain, strengthen your hands and arms to hold the club. You are "set" at both ends of the swing.

Tempo

TEMPO DEALS WITH THE RATE OF SPEED IN your swing. You can still say "Set" and "Swing" yet vary the tempo faster or slower. Go back to the drill in the doorway. Vary the speed faster or slower, depending on your personality or what the shot calls for. Nick Price and Lanny Wad-kins have fast tempos, but Fred Couples has a slow tempo. Yours should be somewhere in between, but it has to suit you. You haven't changed the rhythm, but the tempo can vary, fast or slow.

Timing

THE TIMING OF THE CLUB IN TURNING FROM the right hip to the left creates the curve of the ball. If the timing is such that the clubface is slightly closed and comes in contact with the ball on the outside, the result will be a draw. On the other hand, if the timing is such that the clubface is slightly open  and comes in contact with the inside of the ball, the result will be a fade.

Another aspect of timing, which plagues many amateurs, concerns the fat and thin shots. Both shots result from hitting the ball on the upswing. The bottom of the arc on the fat shot and the thin shot comes behind the ball. The fat shot hits the ground first and the thin shot misses the ground and hits the top half of the ball. To alleviate these problems, your timing must be such that the club contacts the ground just beyond the ball.

Friends of Golf

IN 1979, I SENT OUT A DISTRESS CALL TO A GROUP OF LOCAL PEOPLE that I called my Top 100 Club. I was trying to raise money for the UCLA golf program, and I wanted one hundred peo-

ple to give me $100 each to help jump-start building the program. When I started as men's coach in 1975, the total budget for the golf program was $6,000—scholarships, equipment, and salaries. When I left in 1989, the budget was $120,000, and we were raising most of that ourselves.

In the beginning, we'd bring the college players and pair them, pro-am style, with the contributors. The participants would pay $300 or so to play and would have a chance to interact with the members of the UCLA golf team.

Things grew so much so fast that in 1985 we introduced the idea of an honoree. Lee Trevino, who was the PGA Championship winner, was our first honoree. We had unusual support from companies, hotels, and airlines to contribute prizes for the event and we attracted large numbers of people to the event.

In 1986, Byron Nelson was the honoree, followed by Arnold Palmer, Greg Norman, and Ben Crenshaw. In 1990, we honored two players: Raymond Floyd and Hale Irwin. A confluence of events occurred that year that led to an interesting meeting of people.

The USGA and Karsten Manufacturing were at war over square grooves in irons, and the litigation was heated and vitriolic. So in my fiendish best, I decided to help the cause by pairing Karsten Solheim and USGA president Grant Spaeth along with PGA of America president Pat Reilly, who was the pro at nearby Annandale. I wanted to see if they could walk down the fairway and solve their differences and leave the courts out of it.

Of course, it didn't work, but it was worth trying. But

during the course of the event, something positive did happen. Spaeth played with Hale Irwin, who had won two U.S. Opens and was not exempt for the 1991 Open at Medinah. As a result, Spaeth convinced the USGA to grant Irwin a special exemption. The rest is history: Irwin won his third Open.

The Friends of Golf is a very big reason why I believe that my more than forty years at Bel-Air have been a very special opportunity to give back to golf. The game has been unusually good to me. It has provided me with a fine living, unparalleled experience, and a wealth of lifelong friends. If I have the time and wherewithal to give something in return, I relish it. Joining me in this quest are the honorees since Floyd and Irwin: Jack Nicklaus, Chi Chi Rodriguez, Dave Stockton, Ken Venturi, Tom Weiskopf, Ben Hogan, Johnny Miller, Deane Beman, Sam Snead, Peter Jacobsen, Jim Murray, Tom Lehman, Mark O'Meara, Fred Couples, Corey Pavin, Tony Jacklin, Billy Casper, Amy Alcott, Tommy Bolt, Bob Rosburg, Duffy Waldorf, Scott Simpson, Al Geiberger, and Paul Runyan.

I am now pro emeritus at Bel-Air, and that can mean a couple of things. It might mean that I was put out to pasture. But I choose to look at it as a chance to do things that might be more important than anything I've ever done before. That's why we are making more of a concerted push to get my teaching philosophy before the public. That's where I feel most valuable, sharing my years of experience teaching golf to players who just want to get better, like we all do.

You've gathered by now what my teaching philosophy is. My life philosophy is about giving. It's essential, in my opinion, that you must give without strings or expectations. If you do so, it comes back in ways you never expect. In the final analysis that is how we are measured.

The work I do is not a chore; I enjoy it. If I never played another round of golf, I've played enough and I'd be fine. But I never get enough of teaching. I want to do it until I drop because I'm helping people help themselves. No, we don't have a cure for cancer, but we can help our fellow man.

In this world that's full of stress and turmoil, we have something we can do to help people temporarily leave the difficult things behind. If we can help them enjoy themselves, we've done something worthwhile.

I hope you think so, too.

The Nineteenth Hole

MY ODYSSEY IS IN ITS FINAL STAGES, WITH PERHAPS THE BEST YET to come. Whatever unfolds, the journey has been storybook.

Reels of tape recordings for Mike Purkey covered all the facets of my career. I attempted to include the name, rank, and serial number of every person, thing, and event meaningful in my career.

Unfortunately, show business calls for important documents to be left on the cutting-room floor. Mike did his best to include as much as possible within the alloted time and space. I apologize for leaving anyone out. You are very important to me!

Special appreciation to the club members at the wonderful clubs where I have served and to the club managers, golf professionals, superintendents, caddies, and club workers. You are the best.

To the superb architects, golf professionals, teachers, and coaches I have known, you are a tremendous credit to your profession and I have such respect for your talent and dedication. The media writers and broadcasters have been so meaningful to me.

Special tribute to Joseph C. Dey Jr., a man whose influence on the game over the past seventy years has been so revered.

He was great inspiration for the Little Pro! Tour Commissioners Deane Beman and Tim Fincham have improved markedly under his direction. They have taken his baton and have performed admirably. Beman, in his twenty years as commissioner, achieved monumental things on behalf of the PGA Tour and its members.

The game of golf is fortunate to have organizations like the USGA and the PGA upholding the tenets of the game. I have relished my opportunity to interface with both and have great respect for their dedication. The R&A is likewise such a beacon, as is the Western Golf Association.

My fellow golf professionals, male and female, have been most enjoyable associates. My own assistant professionals and my former employees greatly contributed to my career path. I am forever thankful for them.

So many events in my life provided such substance. Junior Golf, Amateur Golf, College Golf, Professional Golf, Northwood, LSU, Merion, Rockaway Hunt, Thunderbird, Westchester, Bel-Air, the Tour, PGA, USGA, NCAA, *Golf Digest, Golf Magazine,* the Dream Team, FOG, UCLA, the Bubsy, People to People, the Toyota Family Reunion, the WCC, my faith.

People are special in anyone's career. It is not possible to list them all. However, these individuals have been special to me and have not been mentioned previously in this book: Tom Addis, Bob Anderson, Dana Anderson, Dave Anderson, John Anderson, Ron Balicki, Mark Barbato, Charles Bartlett, Dean Beck, Furman Bisher, P. J. Boatwright, Paul Bogin, Gus Brigantino, Lou Costello, A. Ross Crane, Pete

Dalis, David Diltz, Vin Draddy, David Fay, Bob Fischer, Mitch Fox, Leo Fraser, Richard Ghent, M. Donald Grant, Frank Hannegan, Mac Hunter, Charles Jawetz, Gordon Jeffrey, J. T. Jones, Clifford Klenk, Don Klosterman, Jim Mahoney, Roger Maxwell, Jim McDowell, Robert Monsted, G. V. Montgomery, Jerry Perenchio, Dave Podas, Jerry Pyle, Robert Roos, Jeff Rude, Tom Shannon, David Smith, Dick Smith, Ray Snyder, Art Spander, Paul Spengler, Albert Stall, Ed Steidle, Brian Sullivan, Uki Togo, Peter Ueberroth, Chuck VanLing, Carl Walters, Lincoln Werden, Herbert Warren Wind. I would also like to thank the sportswriters at the *Los Angeles Times,* who have always supported me and treated me fairly. And all of the girls, women, and ladies I have known to do with my career!

These supporters have answered the call with the Little Pro in an endearing way. Their caring has been demonstrated uniquely: Ely Callaway, Gerard Cappello, Scott Cook, George Davis Sr., George Davis Jr., Morley Drucker, Tom Fazio, Richard Helmstetter, Barron Hilton, Javier Holtz, Robert Husband, Roberto Lebrija, Howard Lester, Hoot McInerney, Robert McKee, Umberto Neri, Greg Penske, Allard Roen, John Stevenson, Chris Sullivan, Alberto Valenzuela, Richard Wells, and Lance Zuckerbraun.

Whomever I oversighted in the listings, please recognize your importance to me and accept my sincerest apology. This round played through my life with cap, cleats, clubs, courses, and caddies has been shared with incomparable company. I am pleased to share these times with you.

Appreciation to my writer, Mike Purkey, who, by the way,

is a fine player, and special talents Mark Frost and Tim Rosaforte. Agents Barry Weiner and Janis Donnaud have been so helpful. Judith Curr at Simon & Schuster has been great to work with, and she has quite a swing. Kudos to her associates, Peter Borland and Co. Mason Merrins has been a great partner and project coordinator.

Lastly, those who have played with and taught me the most are my own family: Lisa, our sons Michael and Mason, and our daughter, Randy. They never cease to amaze. God bless!

Visit Eddie Merrins at www.swingthehandle.com or www.eddiemerrins.com.

There you may purchase his original instructional book, *Swing the Handle, Not the Clubhead,* written with Dick Aultman, as well as his two instructional video series: *Swing the Handle Video Collection* and *Ben Hogan's Five Lessons: The Modern Fundamentals of Golf.*